Heinrich Gillardon

**Shelleys Einwirkung auf Byron**

Heinrich Gillardon

**Shelleys Einwirkung auf Byron**

ISBN/EAN: 9783744655446

Hergestellt in Europa, USA, Kanada, Australien, Japan

Cover: Foto ©ninafisch / pixelio.de

Weitere Bücher finden Sie auf **www.hansebooks.com**

# Shelley's

# Einwirkung auf Byron

von

## HEINRICH GILLARDON.

**Karlsruhe.**
Druck von M. Gillardon.
1898.

# Seinen Lehrern

Professor Dr. **Hoops** und Professor Dr. **Neumann**

in dankbarer Verehrung

**Der Verfasser.**

# Inhalt

# Bekanntwerden Shelley's und Byron's und ihre perſönlichen Beziehungen.

Es ſoll im folgenden meine Aufgabe ſein den Einfluß Shelley's auf Byron zu unterſuchen, ſoweit er ſich in des letztern Werken verfolgen läßt. Daß Byron in ſeiner Dichtung und in ſeinen Ideen von Shelley beeinflußt wurde, darauf wurde ſchon oft hingewieſen. Bereits Moore hat es in Kapitel XXVII ſeiner Biographie Byron's in „Byron's Life and Letters" gethan. Der Einfluß Shelley's auf Byron datiert von der Zeit ihres perſönlichen Bekanntwerdens am Genfer See. Die beiden Dichter lernten ſich hier im Mai des Jahres 1816 kennen. Sie wurden ſchnell mit einander ſehr gut befreundet, kamen tag-täglich zuſammen, machten gemeinſame Fahrten auf dem See und Ausflüge in die Umgebung und verbrachten oft ganze Nächte in Unterhaltung. Es fand infolgedeſſen naturgemäß ein ſehr reger Ideen-austauſch zwiſchen ihnen ſtatt, der auf Byron ſehr befruchtend wirkte. Dieſer rege perſönliche Verkehr war wohl ausſchlag-gebend für die Einwirkung Shelley's; ohne ihn wäre dieſe vielleicht gar nicht, — oder ſicher nicht in dem Maße, in dem es der Fall war, zu Stande gekommen. Die am Genfer See angeknüpften perſönlichen Beziehungen und mit ihnen der rege Gedanken-Austauſch dauerten fort bis zu dem frühen Tode Shelley's. Von einem ihrer ſpätern Zuſammentreffen ſchreibt dieſer u. a. an ſeine Frau in den Letters from Italy (Brief 77):

— — — we talk, read, etc, untilsix; then we ride, and dine at eight; and after dinner sit talking till four or five in the morning.

für die Art, wie der Ideenaustausch zwischen den beiden Dichtern stattfand, besitzen wir ein wichtiges Dokument in Shelley's „Julian und Maddalo." Shelley schildert uns in diesem Gedicht ein philosophisches Gespräch zwischen zwei Freunden ähnlich den Unterredungen, die 1818 zwischen ihm und Byron zu Venedig stattfanden. Unter Count Maddalo ist Byron, unter Julian er selbst zu verstehen. Da uns die Dichtung wertvolle Fingerzeige für die vorliegende Untersuchung giebt, will ich etwas näher auf sie eingehen. Es heißt da von dem Gespräch der beiden Dichter:

Julian and Maddalo 39 ff.

                              'twas forlorn,
Yet pleasing, such as once, so poets tell.
The devils held within the dales of Hell,
Concerning God, freewill and destiny:
Of all that earth has been or yet may be,
All that vain men imagine or believe.
Or hope can paint or suffering may achieve,
We descanted, and I (for ever still
Is it not wise to make the best of ill?)
Argued against despondency, but pride
Made my companion take the darker side.
The sense that he was greater than his kind
Had struck, methinks, his eagle spirit blind
By gazing on its own exceeding light.

Gott, freier Wille, Vergangenheit und Zukunft unseres Planeten, das Glauben, Hoffen und Leiden der Menschheit sind also die Gegenstände ihrer Unterhaltung. Shelley charakterisiert und begründet hierbei zugleich vortrefflich die pessimistische Art Byron's.

Auf ihrer abendlichen Fahrt über die Lagunen Venedigs kommen die beiden Dichter dann in die Nähe eines gefängnisartigen Hauses, in dem Geisteskranke eingeschlossen sind. Sie hören gerade den Klang der Glocke der die Unglücklichen zum Abendgebet ruft. Julian-Shelley ruft hierbei mit herber Ironie (111 ff.):

As much skill as need to pray
In thanks or hopes for their dark lot have they
To their stern maker.

Es ist dieselbe Entrüstung über die elende Ordnung der Dinge im Menschenleben, die ihn bereits in Queen Mab und in Laon and Cythna den christlichen Gott, als Urheber der bestehenden Ordnung, als Prinzip des Bösen darstellen ließ, wie er es später in „Prometheus" mit Juppiter that. Byron's Darstellung des Gottes der Bibel in „Kain" wurde von dieser Auffassung Shelley's beeinflußt.

Die Erwiderung Maddalo · Byron's ist charakteristisch für seinen Pessimismus, aber zugleich auch für den hohen Flug seiner Wünsche und Gedanken:

And such . . is our mortality,
And this must be the emblem and the sign
Of what should be eternal and divine! —
And like that black and dreary bell, the soul
Hung in a heaven-illumined tower, must toll
Our thoughts and our desires to meet below
Round the rent heart and pray — as madmen do
For what? they know not, till the night of death
As sunset that strange vision, severeth
Our memory from itself, and us from all
We sought and yet were baffled.

Am nächsten Morgen besucht Julian · Shelley wieder Maddalo · Byron und nimmt das am Abend abgebrochene Gespräch wieder auf. Er wendet sich gegen den schwarzen Pessimismus, den Maddalo · Byron in seinen letzten Worten ausgesprochen hat und sagt (139 f.):

The words you spoke last night might well have cast
A darkness on my spirit — — —

Aber — fährt er dann fort:

Mine is another faith — — —
—— — —— —— — —— it is our will
That thus enchains us to permitted ill —
We might be otherwise — we might be all
We dream of, happy, high, majestical.
Where is the love, beauty and truth we seek
But in our mind? and if we were not weak
Should we be less in deed than in desire?

Maddalo · Byron wirft dagegen ein:

Aye, if we were not weak — and we aspire
How vainly to be strong!

Doch Julian · Shelley läßt sich durch diesen Einwurf
nicht beirren, sondern fährt fort:

— — — and those who try may find
How strong the chains are which our spirit bind
Brittle perchance as straw. . . . . We are assured
Much may be conquered, much may be endured
Of what degrades and crushes us. We know
That we have power over ourselves to do
And suffer — what, we know not till we try.

Diese letzten Stellen sind für die Eigenart der beiden
Dichter sehr kennzeichnend. Byron's Realismus läßt den
Gegensatz zwischen Idee und Wirklichkeit, da er sich zu
wenig über diese erheben und von ihr abstrahieren kann,
unversöhnt, während Shelley's Idealismus in der Welt der
Ideen ein höheres und befriedigendes Dasein findet.

Shelley bildet so mit seinem Optimismus und Idealismus einen glücklichen Gegensatz zu dem Realismus und
Pessimismus Byron's. Gerade für diesen Gegensatz zwischen
beiden ist auch die Art wie sie ihr „Ich" in ihren
Dichtungen zu idealisieren pflegen charakteristisch. Shelley
thut es immer nach der besten — idealen Seite hin, Byron
nach der schlechtesten.

Auf der andern Seite fehlt aber auch eine gewisse
Wahlverwandtschaft zwischen ihnen nicht. Beider Charaktere
sind sehr impulsiv, und sie stimmen überein in ihrer Liebe
zur Natur und zur Freiheit.

Wie gesagt, wurde die Einwirkung Shelley's auf Byron
zum großen Teil durch den persönlichen Verkehr bedingt
und hervorgerufen. Mit dieser unmittelbar persönlichen
Einwirkung ging die litterarische durch Shelley's Dichtung
naturgemäß Hand in Hand. Neben philosophischen bilden
litterarische Fragen einen der Hauptgegenstände ihrer Unterhaltung. So sagt Shelley in Brief 76:

We talked a great deal of poetry and such matters last night.

Jeder von beiden kannte, interessierte sich für und kritisierte die Dichtungen des andern. Shelley schreibt u. a. an Leigh Hunt in Brief 83:

Before this you will have seen „Adonais". Lord Byron, I suppose from modesty on account of his being mentioned in it, did not say a word of „Adonais" though he was loud in his praise of „Prometheus"; and, what you will not agree with him in censure of the „Cenci" Certainly, if „Marino Faliero" is a drama, the „Cenci" is not: but that between ourselves.

Ausführlicher auf die persönlichen Beziehungen der beiden Dichter einzugehen, halte ich nicht für nötig, da sich in jeder einigermaßen gründlichen Biographie genügende Angaben darüber finden.

Shelley hat Byron nach zwei Richtungen hin vornehmlich beeinflußt: Erstens indem er auf die Weltanschauung wie sie dieser in seinen Dichtungen aussprach einwirkte — zweitens indem er ihm eine Reihe von Motiven für seine Dichtung gab. Ich will zuerst Shelley's Einwirkung auf Byron's Weltanschauung behandeln. Zum bessern Verständnis schicke ich eine kurze Darstellung der Weltanschauung Byron's bis zu seinem Bekanntwerden mit Shelley im Jahre 1816 voraus. Ich folge hier der Darstellung Donner's in seiner Abhandlung „Lord Byron's Weltanschauung."

---

Kapitel II.

## Die Einwirkung Shelley's auf Byron's Weltanschauung.

Byron's Weltanschauung war bis zum Prayer of Nature (1806) christlich. Er wendet sich hier zum ersten Male von der christlichen Weltanschauung ab und huldigt einer Art Deismus. Diesen Wandel schreibt Donner dem

Einfluß Rousseau's und Locke's zu. Byron kehrte nach
diesem Bruch mit seinen alten Anschauungen nicht mehr zu
ihnen zurück. Es begann für ihn nun das Ringen und
Kämpfen nach einer neuen Wahrheit, das bis zu seinem
Lebensende dauerte, ohne daß es ihm gelang sie zu finden.
Die Folge davon ist sein Skeptizismus, der uns in seiner
Dichtung in verschiedenen Stadien der Entwicklung und in
verschiedenen Erscheinungsformen entgegentritt. Von diesem
Skeptizismus sagt dann Donner am Schluß seiner Aus-
führungen (Seite 138):

„Wohl bleibt Byron in seiner späteren Skepsis
unschlüssig stehn. Vor der Beantwortung mancher Fragen
bebt er zurück, nicht als ob er fürchtete, mit der Tradition
allzu jäh zu brechen, sondern weil er die Unmöglichkeit
erkannte, zu den höchsten Höhen des Gedankens, zu den
tiefsten Geheimnissen des Daseins emporzuringen. Aus dieser
schon früh geahnten Unmöglichkeit fließt die höchste Stufe
des Weltschmerzes her und bleibt unversöhnt."

So ganz recht hat Donner mit dieser Behauptung
nicht. Byron. hat den Weltschmerz überwunden oder er war
wenigstens auf dem Wege dies zu thun durch — die Resignation.
Es scheint mir dies aus einer allerdings vereinzelten Stelle
erschlossen werden zu können, wo er eine solche Resignation
ausspricht;

Sardanapalus Act II, 1.

There's something sweet in my uncertainty
I would not change for your Chaldean lore
Besides I know of these all clay can know
Of aught above it or below it — nothing
I see their brilliancy and feel their beauty
When they shine on my grave I shall know neither.

Während wir nun in Byron's Dichtung als Ausfluß
seines Skeptizismus ein beständiges Hin- und Herschwanken
zwischen zum Teil oft entgegengesetzten Ansichten finden,
sehen wir ihn im zweiten Teil von Gesang III C.H. mit
dem Feuer eines Neubekehrten eine Art pantheistischen
Naturkultus verkündigen. Die betreffenden Stellen zeigen

deutlich), daß Byron hier im Besitz einer neugewonnenen Weltanschauung ist, die ihm Befriedigung und Genugthuung giebt und für ihn eine Art neuer positiver Überzeugung ist. Pantheistischen Anschauungen begegnen wir seit dieser Zeit fortwährend in Byron's Dichtung, doch nehmen sie nie wieder einen so breiten Raum ein als im zweiten Teil des dritten Gesanges von C.H., der fast ausschließlich aus einer Reihe pantheistischer Hymnen auf die Natur besteht. Infolgedessen hebt sich diese Episode in der innern Entwicklung Byron's scharf von seinem vorausgehenden und folgenden Skeptizismus ab.

Wie kam Byron zu dieser neuen Anschauung? Durch sein lebhaftes Naturgefühl war er jedenfalls zum Pantheismus prädisponiert (vgl. Donner S. 112); aber bis zum Jahre 1816 zeigen sich nur unbedeutende Spuren davon in seiner Dichtung. Die Naturbeseelungen in seinen früheren Dichtungen sind wie Donner richtig bemerkt (S. 111) lediglich aus Byron's Naturgefühl hervorgegangen. Die Ansätze zum Pantheismus in den Hebrew melodies 1815, besonders in dem Lied »When coldness wraps this suffering clay« sind so unbestimmt und so fragwürdiger Natur, daß man darauf keine großen Schlüsse auf Byron's Pantheismus vor dem Jahre 1816 bauen kann.

Mit Spinoza beschäftigte er sich allerdings schon im Jahre 1811 und mit Wordsworth's pantheistischer Natur-dichtung war er sicher schon lang vor 1816 bekannt, aber keiner von beiden hatte befruchtend auf seine Dichtung gewirkt. Es ist nun sicher in psychologischer Hinsicht eine höchst auffällige Thatsache, daß sich die schwachen und unbestimmten Keime von Byron's Pantheismus im zweiten Teil von C.H. Gesang III zu einem ausgebildeten System entwickelt haben, während sich selbst in der ersten Hälfte des betreffenden Gesanges gar keine Spuren davon finden. Aus der Latenz des Pantheismus in Byron infolge seines Naturgefühls und durch den Einfluß Spinoza's, Wordworth's und andere litterarische Einflüsse läßt sich dieses plötzliche und mächtige Erscheinen des Pantheismus nicht begreifen.

Diese konnten wohl als fördernde Faktoren mitwirken, aber ausschlaggebend waren sie nicht, denn sonst hätte die Entwicklung bei Byron unbedingt langsamer, organischer und vorbereiteter sein müssen. Es bedurfte also eines Anstoßes von außen um den latenten Pantheismus Byron's zu entwickeln — und dieser Anstoß kam von Shelley. Ich will damit nicht sagen, daß ich die ganze pantheistische Naturdichtung Byron's auf Shelley zurückführen will. Shelley selbst zeigt sich in seiner Naturdichtung stark von dem Altmeister der englischen Naturdichtung, von Wordsworth beeinflußt. Besonders zeigt sich der Einfluß Wordsworth's in den ums Jahr 1816 entstandenen Dichtungen Shelley's, vor allem „Alastor" und „Montblanc". Shelley beschäftigte sich aufs angelegentlichste mit Wordsworth's Dichtung während des Schweizeraufenthalts vom Jahre 1816 und machte bei Byron eifrig Propaganda dafür. Dieser bekam von ihm Wordsworth's Naturpoesie bis um Überdruß zu kosten.

Shelley's wie Byron's Dichtungen aus dieser Zeit zeigen infolgedessen eine Menge Anklänge an Wordsworth, auf die ich jedoch nicht im einzelnen eingehen kann. Ob Wordsworth's Naturdichtung ohne Shelley's Vermittlung jemals einen bedeutenden Einfluß auf Byron gehabt hätte, scheint mir zum mindesten fraglich, besonders bei dessen Geringschätzung für Wordsworth's Dichtung, die er öfter ausspricht; einmal geht er sogar soweit sie geradezu als „trash" zu bezeichnen. So aber gehn bisweilen der Einfluß Shelley's und der Wordsworth's Hand in Hand und da Shelley selbst in seiner pantheistischen Naturdichtung stark von Wordsworth beeinflußt ist, ist es oft unmöglich fest-zustellen, welcher von beiden auf Byron gewirkt hat. Ich bin deshalb genötigt, wo neben Shelley's Einfluß der Wordworth's hergegangen sein kann, auch dessen Dichtung mit in den Bereich meiner Untersuchung zu ziehen.

Shelley hatte für sein pantheistisches Evangelium einen mächtigen Bundesgenossen in der umgebenden Natur — in der gewaltigen Alpenwelt, die in ihrer erhabenen Größe und Majestät wie geschaffen war zum Tempel einer pantheiſtiſchen Gottesverehrung. Schon Gray ſchrieb in einem Brief an Weſt während ſeiner Reiſe in den Alpen:

Not a precepice, not a torrent not a cliff, but is pregnant with religion and poetry (16 Nov. 1739).

Ähnliches hat Byron empfunden und in CH III. 91 ausgeſprochen:

Not vainly did the early Persian make
His altar the high places and the peak
Of earth overgazing mountains and thus take
A fit and unwalled temple, there to seek
The Spirit in whose honour shrines are weak
Upreared of human hands. Come and compare
Columns and idol dwellings, Goth or Greek
With Nature's realms of worship earth and air
Nor fix on fond abodes to circumscribe thy pray'r!

Einen ähnlichen Gedanken hatte Byron bereits im Prayer of Nature (1806) geäußert.

Shall man confine his Maker's sway
To Gothic domes of mouldering stone?
Thy temple is the face of day;
Earth, ocean, heaven thy boundless throne.

Byron hat dieſe Zeilen in Nachahmung Pope's gedichtet. Er denkt ſich hier die Gottheit noch perſönlich, während er ſie in der Stelle CH III 91, als den in der Natur waltenden Geiſt, als Naturkraft auffaßt. Dieſe Auffaſſung deckt ſich mit der von Shelley in Queen Mab I 264 ausgeſprochenen.

Spirit of Nature! here!
In this interminable wilderness
Of worlds, at whose immensity
Even soaring fancy staggers,
Here is thy fitting temple.

Vorbild zu der Stelle in Child Harold war jedoch wohl Excursion IV 671 ff.:

— — — the Persian zealous to reject
Altar and image and the inclusive walls

And roofs of temples built by human hands —
To loftiest heights ascending, from their tops,
With myrtle wreathed tiara on his brow
Presented sacrifice to moon and stars,
And to winds and mother elements,
And the whole circle of heavens for him
A sensitive existence and a God
With lifted hands invoked, and songs of praise.

Wie bereits erwähnt tritt der Pantheismus in Byron's späterer Dichtung nie wieder so stark hervor wie im zweiten Teil von C. H. III. Auf mich machen die pantheistischen Natur-ergüsse, die sich hier finden den Eindruck, als ob sie in einer Art Ekstase geschrieben worden seien — eine Ekstase die durch den Enthusiasmus und Mystizismus Shelley's und den über-wältigenden Eindruck der umgebenden Natur hervorgerufen wurde. Byron selbst schreibt über seine damalige Stimmung in einem Brief an Moore vom 28. Jan. 1817 (Venedig):

I was half mad during the time of its composition (nämlich C. H. III) between metaphysics, mountains, lakes, love unextinguishable, thoughts unutterable, and the nightmare of my own delinquencies.

Kein Wunder, daß sich Byron's pantheistischer Natur-Enthusiasmus bald abkühlte und nicht zu seiner dauernden Weltanschauung wurde. Die Beeinflussung derselben durch Shelley im Einzelnen zu untersuchen soll zunächst meine Aufgabe sein.

Hierzu ist es nötig einige allgemeine Bemerkungen über Shelley's Weltanschauung vorauszuschicken.

Shelley's Weltanschauung ist durchaus nicht einheitlich. Die pantheistischen Ideen sind in ihr zwar vorherrschend, daneben finden sich aber auch deistische und dualistische Elemente. Selbst sein Pantheismus ist nicht der Ausdruck eines einheitlichen Systems. Neben dem Pantheismus Spinoza's findet sich der Spiritualismus Berkeley's. Auch Plato und Shaftesbury haben auf die Gestaltung der Weltanschauung Shelley's Einfluß gehabt.

Dieses Neben· und Durcheinander von verschiedenen philosophischen Systemen mag etwas sonderbar erscheinen, aber wir müssen in Betracht ziehen, daß Shelley in erster Linie Dichter und als solcher Eklektiker und nicht Philosoph war, der alles auf eine abstrakte formel zurückzuführen versucht. Im Gegensatz zu Byron, dessen Weltanschauung fortwährenden Veränderungen und Modifikationen unter- worfen war, steht die Shelley's ungefähr seit 1815 ziemlich fest. Manchen von seinen Ideen giebt er erst verhältnismäßig spät in seiner Dichtung Ausdruck, so daß einige Male der fall eintrat, daß Byron sie vor ihm dichterisch verwertete. Ich werde deshalb dann und wann genötigt sein um den Einfluß Shelley's nachzuweisen Stellen aus dessen Dichtung anzuführen die nach den betreffenden in der Byron's entstanden sind. Doch sind diese Stellen so in der Art Shelley's gedichtet, daß man sofort dessen Vaterschaft erkennt.

Eine ausführliche Darstellung der Weltanschauung Shelley's zu geben, halte ich nicht für notwendig; ich werde im folgenden nur die Punkte berühren, von denen aus ein Einfluß auf Byron stattgefunden hat und diesen unmittelbar im Anschluß daran behandeln.

Mit Spinoza sind für Shelley Gott und Natur gleichbedeutend. So sagt er in seiner Prosa-Abhandlung A refutation of Deism (S. 78.):

The distinction between the Universe, and that by which the Universe is upheld, is manifestly erroneous. — · — — — In the language of reason the words God and Universe are synonymous.

Ähnlich sagt er in Laon and Cythna V 51:

O Spirit vast and deep as Night and Heaven!
Mother and soul of all to which is given
The light of life, the loveliness of being

Nature, or God, or Love

Wir finden in dieser Stelle fast die ganze An- schauung Shelley's von der Substanz ausgesprochen. Es ist eine poetische Gestaltung der Lehre Spinoza's.

Die Substanz ist der Grund aller Dinge; sie ist der Quell des Lebens, und als solche faßt sie Shelley als Weltliebe auf; alles ist durch sie bedingt; sie ist demnach das Weltgesetz oder die Weltnotwendigkeit (necessity).

Die Substanz ist ferner ihrer Natur nach unendlich; sie ist nicht nur in den Lebewesen die Quelle des Lebens, sondern sie ist in dem ganzen gewaltigen All der Natur verbreitet und durchdringt es. So spricht Shelley in der Abhandlung „On the Devil, and Devils" von der omnipresence of God, pervading the infinity of space and being. Ähnlich sagt er in Queen Mab I 264 ff:

Spirit of Nature! Here!
In this interminable wilderness
Of worlds, at whose immensity
Even soaring fancy staggers,
Here is thy fitting temple.
Yet not the slightest leaf
That quivers to the passing breeze
Is less instinct with thee:
Yet not the meanest worm
That lurks in graves and fattens on the dead
Less shares thy eternal breath

Von dieser Anschauung ist Byron offenbar in C H III, 89 beeinflußt, wenn er sagt:

— — — — From the high host
Of stars, to the lulled lake and mountain coast
All is concentred in a life intense
Where not a beam, nor air, nor leaf is lost,
But has a part of being and a sense
Of that which is of all Creator and defence,

Donner hat auf Seite 118 seiner Abhandlung bereits auf die Übereinstimmung dieser beiden Stellen hingewiesen. Dieselbe Vorstellung findet sich späterhin noch bei Byron Island II, 16:

— — — — — Are the waves
Without a spirit? Are the dropping caves
Without a feeling — — — —

Die Anschauung von der alldurchdringenden allbelebenden Substanz findet sich auch bei Wordsworth. So Excursion IV 427 ff:

Theſe craggy regions, these chaotic wilds
Does that benignity pervade, that warms
The mole contented with her darksome walk
In the cold ground and to the emmet gives
Her foresight and intelligence. — — --

Ähnlich ſpricht er von ihr in Lines, composed above Tintern Abbey 97 ff. als:

the being,
Whose dwelling is the light of setting suns
And the round ocean, and the living air,
And the blue sky, and in the mind of man;
A motion and a spirit, that impels
All thinking things, all objects of all thoughts
And rolls through all things

ferner in The old Cumberland beggar (1798). Excursion IX 1 ff.

Neben dem Einfluß Shelley's kann hier also auch der Wordworth's gewirkt haben.

Direkt als Quelle des Lebens bezeichnet Shelley die Subſtanz in Adonais XXXVIII

— — — but the pure spirit shall flow
Back to the burning fountain whence it came.

Dieſelbe Metapher von der Gottheit gebraucht er in Essay on Christianity (1815?) wenn er ſpricht von:

The unobscured irradiations from the fountain-
fire all goodness.

Die gleiche Anſchauung findet ſich bei Byron Sar-danapalus II, 1:

— — — thou true sun!
The burning oracle of all that live,
As fountain of all life, and symbol of
Him who bestows it, — -- — --

Da Byron's Sardanapalus um dieſelbe Zeit wie Shelley's Adonais entſtand (1821), ist deſſen Einfluß immerhin möglich. Näher liegt allerdings ſeine Faſſung der von Thomson in der „Hymn" ausgeſprochenen:

2

Great source of day! best image here below
Of thy Creator.

Zurück geht dieser Vergleich wohl auf Plato Republik
VI 508 D.

Da die Substanz das Einzige an sich existierende —
das absolute Sein ist, und alle Daseins- und Lebenserscheinungen
aus ihr hervorgehen, so ist sie das Gesetz aller Dinge oder
wie Spinoza sagt: Gott ist die immanente Ursache der
Welt. Die Auffassung von der Substanz als Weltgesetz
spricht Shelley aus in Queen Mab VI 197

Spirit of Nature! all-sufficing Power
Necessity! thou mother of the world!

In der Anmerkung zu dieser Stelle erörtert er diesen
Satz von der Notwendigkeit nach allen Seiten hin. Es
finden sich in Queen Mab noch mehrere Parallelstellen zu
der oben zitierten.

Ferner in Laon and Cythna IX, 27 wo die Weltnotwendigkeit als ethisches Gesetz aufgefaßt wird

Necessity, whose sightless strength forever
Evil with evil, good with good must bind

und in A refutation of Deism (1814) wo die Notwendigkeit
als Naturgesetz erscheint:

The greatest even with the smallest motions of
the universe are subjected to the rigid necessity of
inevitable laws.

Nach Shelley hat Byron den gleichen Gedanken im
Deformed Transformed (1824) I, 2 ausgesprochen.

The planet wheels till it becomes
A comet and destroying as it sweeps
The stars, goes out. The poor worm winds its way
Living upon the death of other things,
But still like them must live and die, the subject
Of something which has made it.
You must obey what all obey, the rule'
Of fixed necessity: against her edict
Rebellion prospers not.

Diese Stelle ist außerdem noch durch die bereits aus Queen Mab (I, 126) angeführte beeinflußt: die Weltkraft wirkt in gleicher Weise auf das mächtige Himmelsgestirn, wie auf den armseligen Wurm. Auch eine Stelle aus Shelley's Epipsychidion (1821) hat sichtbar auf die Gestaltung der vorliegenden mitgewirkt. Es heißt dort 368 ff.

Thou too, o Comet beautiful and fierce
Who drew the heart of this frail Universe
Towards thine own, till, wreckt in that convulsion,
Alternating attraction and repulsion,
Thine went astray, and that was rent in twain,

Die Sterne spielen eine ziemlich große Rolle in Shelley's Dichtung. Byron wurde in dieser Hinsicht besonders im „Kain" von ihm beeinflußt. Ich werde hierauf in anderm Zusammenhange zurückkommen. Eine Parallele zu der oben angeführten Stelle aus Deformed Transformed findet sich Kain II, 1, wo allerdings wohl mehr an die Vorsehung in christlichem Sinne als an Shelley's Notwendigkeit gedacht wird:

The little shining fire-fly in its flight
And the immortal star in its great course,
Must both be guided.

Daß Byron mit Shelley Gott als Weltgesetz und als immanente Ursache der Welt betrachtet geht aus seiner Darstellung des Gottes der Bibel in Kain hervor. Er kann zwar diese Ansicht direkt aus Spinoza haben, da er sich zur Zeit der Entstehung Kain's (1821) mit dem Amsterdamer Philosophen beschäftigte, da aber der Gott der Bibel auch hier sonst noch Züge hat, die auf die originelle Auffassung Shelley's von ihm zurückgehen so bin ich geneigt auch hier seinen Einfluß anzunehmen. Die Übertragung der Vorstellung von der Substanz als der immanenten Ursache der Welt auf den Gott der Bibel findet sich bei Byron:

Kain I, 1 — — — But He! so wretched in his height
So restless in his wretchedness, must still
Create and recreate.

Heaven and Earth Sc. 3:

**Ask** him who made thee greater than myself
And mine, but not less subject to his own
Almightyness

Da nun alles aus der Notwendigkeit hervorgeht, so giebt es nichts was an sich gut oder schlecht ist, sondern nur was notwendig ist. Gut und schlecht sind zwar im Wesen der Dinge begründet, aber nur zufällige von Fall zu Fall sich ändernde Attribute. So sagt Shelley in dem Prosa-Fragment „On the Punishment of Death": — — — — — that intertexture of good and evil with which Nature seems to have clothed every form of individual existence.

Die gleiche Vorstellung liegt zu Grunde, wenn Luzifer in Kain II, 2 sagt

But ignorance of evil doth noth save
From evil: it must roll on the same,
A part of all things.

Die schaffende Substanz kann sich schöpfend und zerstörend bethätigen (Queen Mab VI 190):

Soul of the Universe! eternal spring
Of life and death, of happiness and woe.

Diese Vorstellung von der Substanz als Lebenerhaltendes und zerstörendes Prinzip hat dann Byron im „Kain" auf den Gott der Bibel übertragen

The Maker — call him
Which name thou wilt; he makes but to destroy
(Kain I, 1)

Ebenso in Heaven and Earth Szene 3:

And the Omnipotent who makes and crushes!

Der Gott der Bibel wird im Kain überhaupt als zerstörendes und dem Menschen feindliches Prinzip aufgefaßt. Die Keime zu dieser Auffassung sind schon im Paradise Lost gegeben. Byron wurde in seinem Kain sicher von der unsterblichen Dichtung Milton's beeinflußt; es finden sich in seiner Dichtung wörtliche Anklänge an Paradise Lost. Auf der andern Seite war jedoch auch Shelley's Einfluß, wie aus dem folgenden hervorgehen wird, für die Gestaltung von „Cain" fehr bedeutend. Schon Moore hat dies erkannt. Es geht dies aus einem Brief Shelley's an Horatio Smith hervor (Brief 96) Shelley schreibt hier u. a.:

Lord Byron has read me one or two letters of Moore to him - - — — -- — -- Amongst other things, however, Moore — — — — — -- seems to deprecate my influence over his mind, on the subject of religion, and to attribute the tone assumed in Cain to my suggestions. — - — - — -- I think you know Moore. Pray, assure him, that I have not the smallest influence over Lord Byron, in this particular, and if I had, I certainly should employ it to eradicate from his great mind the delusions of Christianity, which inspite of his reason, seem perpetually to recur, and to lay in ambush for the hours of sickness and distress.

Diese Stelle ift, da sie von Shelley herrührt, der vielleicht wie kein zweiter das innerste Wesen Byron's erkannte und durchschaute auch hinsichtlich des religiösen Empfindens Byron's interessant. Da Donner nicht auf sie Bezug genommen hat, mache ich hier auf sie aufmerksam.

Ehe ich nun weiter auf die Einwirkung Shelley's auf „Cain" eingehe, muß ich noch einiges über die fernere Ge- staltung seiner Vorstellung von der schaffenden und zerstören- den Substanz vorausschicken.

Shelley hat alle Tribute der Substanz als der zerstörenden Kraft auf den Gott der Bibel übertragen. Er stellt ihn in der poetischen fiktion als Welttyrannen, als Perfonifikation des bösen Prinzips dar, im Gegensatz zur allgütigen Natur, deren ureigenstes Wesen Liebe und harmonie ift, und die somit als gutes Prinzip erscheint. Er kommt so zum Dualismus. Daß der Dualismus eine philosophische Überzeugung für ihn war soll damit nicht gesagt sein. Philosophie und Poesie sind bei ihm in der Regel so eng verknüpft, daß es oft schwer ift beide zu trennen. In dem Prosa-Aufsatz „On the Devil, and the devils" (1815?) unterfucht er die Frage nach der Entstehung der Vorstellung von dem guten und bösen Prinzip nach allen Richtungen hin. Er sagt darüber:

To suppose that the world was created and is now superintended by two spirits of a balanced power and opposite dispositions, is simply a personification of the struggle which we experience within ourselves.

Er sagt dann von der Entstehung der christlichen Vorstellung vom Teufel:

Like panic-stricken slaves in the presence of a jealous and suspicious despot, they have tortured themselves to devise some flattering sophism, by which they might appease him by the most contradictory praises — endeavering to reconcile omnipotence, and benevolence, and equity, in the author of an universe where evil and good are inextricably entangled, and where the most admirable tendencies to happiness and preservation are for ever baffled by misery and decay. The Christians, therefore invented or adopted the Devil to extricate them from this difficulty.

Shelley spricht dann ausführlich von dem Kampf Luzifers und Gottes in der Darstellung der Bibel und der Milton's, von ihrem sonstigen Verhältnis zu einander, von dem vermuthlichen Wohnsitz des Teufels u. s. w.

In seinem Essay on Christianity (1815?) spricht er ebenfalls von dem guten und bösen Prinzip. Es ist also klar daß er sich aufs lebhafteste mit diesen Fragen beschäftigt hat, wohl auch seine Ansichten Byron gegenüber ausgesprochen und diesem so die Anregung zum „Kain", wenigstens in der Gestalt, wie wir ihn jetzt haben gegeben hat. Byron hat sich schon in früheren Jahren mit dem Gedanken einer „Kain" Dichtung getragen, wie dies aus einer Stelle (Cain was conceived many years ago) aus dem bereits angeführten Brief an Horatio Smith hervorgeht, so daß es zu weit gehen hieße die Anregung zum Kain schlechthin auf Shelley zurückzuführen.

Die Vorstellung von den beiden Prinzipen die in ewigem Streit mit einander liegen hat Shelley besonders oft in seiner Dichtung ausgesprochen. So Laon and Cythna I, 25:

Know then, that from the depth of ages old,
Two Powers o'er mortal things dominion hold

Ruling the world with a divided lot,
Immortal, all pervading, manifold,
Twin Genii, equal Gods — when life and thought
Sprang forth, the burst the womb of inessential
Nought.

Diese Stelle war wohl das Vorbild zu der ähnlichen
in „Cain" Akt I Ende, wo Luzifer sagt:

— — — — all things are
Divided with me; life and death — and time —
Eternity — and heaven and earth — and that
Which is not heaven nor earth — — —

Aus dieser Stelle und ähnlichen zu schließen, daß
Byron selbst dem Dualismus gehuldigt habe ist um so
weniger zulässig, da er hier blos eines der poetischen Motive
Shelley's in seine Dichtung aufgenommen hat (vgl. über
den Dualismus Byron's Donner S. 78).

Von dem ewigen Kampf der beiden Prinzipe spricht
Shelley Laon and Cythna 1 26, 27.

The earliest dweller of the world alone,
Stood on the verge of chaos: Lo! afar
O'er the wide wild abyss two meteors shone,
Sprung from the depth of its tempestuous jar: .
A blood red Comet and the Morning Star
Mingling their beams in combat — as he stood,
All thoughts within his mind waged mutualwar,
In dreadful sympathy — when to the flood
That fair star fell, he turned and shed his
brother's blood.

### XXVII.

Thus evil triumphed, and the Spirit of evil
One Power of many shapes which none may know,
One Shape of many names, the Fiend did revel
In victory, reigning o'er a world of woe,
For the new race of man went to and fro
Famished and homeless, loathed and loathing, wild,
And hating good — for his immortal foe,
He changed from starry shape, beauteous and mild,
To a dire snake, with man and beast unreconciled.

Das böſe Prinzip ſiegt alſo; es unterdrückt die Menſchheit, verelendet ſie und macht ſie ſchlecht. In den beiden letzten Zeilen der Stanze ſchwebt Shelley die Darſtellung in Paradise Lost vor. Die Verknüpfung der Blutthat Kain's mit dem Kampf der beiden Prinzipe iſt meines Wiſſens hier neu. Vielleicht bekam Byron durch dieſe Stelle erſt die Konzeption zum „Kain“ in der Geſtalt, wie wir ihn haben, der Gegenſatz der beiden Prinzipe iſt bei ihm die Hauptſache und die Blutthat klappt dann im III. Akt hinten nach, ebenſo unvorbereitet und unmotiviert, wie hier am Ende von Stanze XXVI.

Mögen nun auch die Beziehungen von „Laon and Cythna“ I, 26, 27 zu „Kain“ nicht ſo eng ſein, wie ich angenommen habe, ſo iſt die Einwirkung Shelley's darauf doch auf jeden Fall bedeutend. Das Motiv von den beiden ewig kämpfenden Principen verwendet Byron in Akt II, 2. Er läßt Luzifer hier ſagen:

No! by Heaven, wich He
Holds, and the abyss, and the immensity
Of worlds and life, which I hold with him -- No!
I have a victor — true; but no superior.
Homage he has from all, but none from me.
I battle it against him, as I battled
In highest heaven. Through all eternity
And the unfathomable gulf of Hades,
And the interminable realms of space,
And the infinity of endless ages,
All, all will I dispute! And world by world,
And star by star, and universe by universe
Shall in the balance tremble, till the great
Conflict shall cease, if ever it shall cease,
Which it never shall till He or I be conquered!
And what can quench our immortality?
Our mutual and irrevocable hate?
He as the conqueror will call the conquer'd
Evil; but what will be the good he gives?
Were I the victor his works would be deemed
The only evil ones.

Wie bei Shelley der „Morning Star" (-Luzifer) ist im „Kain" Luzifer der unterliegende und zugleich der bessere Teil. Auch eine andere Stelle im „Kain" ist von Laon und Cythna I, 27, beeinflußt. Das triumphierende Übel wird hier bezeichnet als:

> One Power of many shapes, which none may know,
> One Shape of many names.

Entsprechend heißt es in „Kain" Akt III

> Iehovah upon earth, and God in heaven,
> And it may be with other names, because
> Thine attributes seem many.

Die Attribute des bösen Prinzips werden von Shelley auf den Gott der Bibel übertragen in Queen Mab — es ist dies eines seiner frühesten, dichterischen Motive und fand sich vermutlich schon in seiner nicht mehr erhaltenen Jugend-dichtung „Ahasverus" — und im „Prometheus" auf Jove. Die vornehmlich hier in Betracht kommenden Stellen sind:

Queen Mab VI 96 ff.

> The changing seasons, winter's leafless reign,
> The budding of the heaven-breathing trees,
> The eternal orbs that beautify the night,
> The sun-rise and the setting of the moon,
> Earthquakes and wars and poisons and disease,
> And all their causes, to an abstract point,
> Converging, thou didst bend and called it God!
> The self-sufficing, the omnipotent,
> The merciful, and the avenging God!
> Who, prototype of human misrule, sits
> High in heaven's realm, upon a golden throne,
> Even like an earthly king; and whose dread work,
> Hell, gapes for ever for the unhappy slaves
> Of fate, whom he created in his sport,
> To triumph in their torments, when they fell!
> Earth heard the name, earth trembled, as the smoke
> Of his revenge ascended up to heaven,
> Blotting, the constellations; and the cries
> Of millions, butchered in sweet confidence —

Queen Mab VII 84 ff.

Is there a God? — Aye, an almigthy God
And vengeful as almighty. — Once his voice
Was heard on earth: earth shuddered at the sound;
The fiery-visaged firmament expressed
Abhorrence, and the grave of nature yawned
To swallow all the dauntless and the good
That dared to hurl defiance at his throne,
Girt as it was with power. None but slaves
Survived, — cold-blooded slaves, who did the work
Of tyrannous omnipotence — — —

Queen Mab VII 248 ff.

The unprevailing malice of my foe,
Whose bootless rage heaps torments for the brave,
Adds impotent eternities to pain,
Whilst keenest disappointment racks his breast
To see the smiles of peace around them play,
To frustrate or to sanctify their doom.

In Queen Mab VII 199 wird ferner der Gott der Bibel
als almighty tyrant bezeichnet und in Queen Mab VI 221 als:

almighty fiend,
Whose name usurps thy (nature) honours.

Denselben Motiven begegnen wir in „Laon und Cythna".
Doch würde es mich zu weit führen, auch aus dieser Dichtung die hierher gehörigen Stellen anzuführen. Da „Laon
und Cythna" und Byron's „Prometheus" in dem sich die
oben näher gekennzeichneten Motive auf Juppiter übertragen
finden, um dieselbe Zeit (1816) entstanden sind, so liegt es
nahe, auch hier den Einfluß Shelley's zu vermuten. Im
einzelnen will ich dies erst weiter unten näher ausführen.

Die Attribute des bösen Prinzips hat Shelley dann,
wie es Byron bereits in seinem Gedicht „Prometheus"
gethan hat, in seinem Drama „Prometheus" auf Jove
übertragen. So:

Prometheus Akt I, l, 115 ff.

Mother, thy sons and thou
Scorn him, without whose all-enduring will

Beneath the fierce omnipotence of Jove,
Both they and thou had vanished, like thin mist
Unrolled on the morning wind. Know ye not me,
The Titan? He who made his agony
The barrier to your else all-conquering foe?

\* \*
\*

Why scorns the spirit which informs ye, now
To commune with me? me alone, who checked,
As one who checks a fiend-drawn charioteer,
The falsehood and the force of him who reigns
Supreme, and with the groans of pining slaves
Fills your dim glens and liquid wildernesses.

Prometheus Akt I, 1, 282 ff.

But thou, who art the God and Lord: O, thou
Who fillest with thy soul this world of woe,
To whom all things of Earth and Heaven do bow
In fear and worship: all pervading foe!
I curse thee! let a sufferer's curse
Clasp thee, his torturer, like remorse;
Till thine Infinity shall be
A robe of envenomed agony;
And thine Omnipotence a crown of pain,
To cling like burning gold round thy dissolving brain.
Heap on thy soul by virtue of this Curse,
Ill deeds, then be thou damned, beholding good;
Both infinite as is the universe,
And thou, and thy self-torturing solitude.
An awful image of calm power
Though now thou sittest, let the hour
Come, when thou must appear to be
That which thou art internally.
And after many a false and fruitless crime
Scorn track thy lagging fall thro' boundless space
and time.

Überall wird Gott-Jove hier als Personifikation
der finstern Macht dargestellt, die das Prinzip der Zerstörung,
die Ursache der Unterdrückung und Verelendung der Menschen
ist. In welcher Weise Byron im „Kain" in dieser Hinsicht
von Shelley beeinflußt wurde, ergibt sich ohne weiteres aus
einem Vergleich der oben angeführten Stellen aus Shelley's
Dichtung mit den folgenden aus „Kain".

Kain Akt I, 1.

Souls who dare use their immortality —
Souls who dare look the omnipotent Tyrant in
His ever lasting face, and tell him that
His evil is not good! If he has made,
As he saith — which I know not nor believe —
But if he made us — he can not unmake;
We are immortal! — nay he'd have us so
That he may torture — let him! He is great —
But in his greatness is no happier than
We in our conflict! Goodness would not make
Evil; and what else has he made? But let him
Sit on his vast and solitary throne
Creating worlds, to make eternity
Less burthensome to his immense existence
And unparticipated solitude;
Let him crowd orb on orb: he is alone
Indefinite indissoluble tyrant;
Could he but crush him self, 'twere the best boon
He ever granted: but let him reign on,
And multiply himself in misery!

Zum Teil scheint mir diese Stelle auch Beziehungen
zu haben zu einer in Shelley's Roman »The Assassins«
dessen Entstehung von Forman in das Jahr 1814 gesetzt
wird. Es heißt dort in Kapitel III:

The great tyrant is baffled, even in success. Joy;
joy! to his tortured foe. — — — — Ha! his suicidal
hand might dare as well abolish the mighty
frame of things!

Im folgenden wird dann die Thätigkeit des bösen
Prinzips wieder in der typischen Weise beschrieben, so daß
ich wohl nicht die ganze Stelle anzuführen brauche.

Als weitere Stellen aus „Kain" kommen hier noch
in Betracht

Akt I
— — — — — — as I scorn all
That bows to him, who made things but to bend
Before his sullen sole eternity

Akt I

Higher things than ye are slaves: and higher
Than them or ye would be so, did they not
Prefer an independency of torture
To the smooth agonies of adulation
In hymns and harpings, and self-seeking prayers,
To that which is omnipotent, because
It is omnipotent, and not from love
But terror and selfhope.

Akt II, 2

Why do I exist
Why art thou wretched? why are all things so?
Ev'n he who made us must be, as the maker
Of things unhappy! To produce destruction
Can surely never be the task of joy.

Auch in Heaven and Earth ist die Auffassung des
Gottes der Bibel der in „Kain" ähnlich.

So Heaven and Earth Sc 3:

Why should our hymn be raised, our knees be bent
Before the implacable Omnipotent
Since we must fall the same?
If he hath made earth, let it be his shame,
To make a world for torture.

Daß das böse Prinzip der Unterdrücker der menschlichen
Freiheit und des menschlichen Gedankens ist (vgl. Shelley
Queen Mab VI 96 ff. Laon and Cythna II, 8) spricht Byron
an folgenden Stellen aus:

Kain Akt I, 1

— My father is
Tamed down; my mother has forgot the mind
Which made her thurst for knowledge at the risk
Of an eternal curse — — —

Kain Akt I, 1                                                    [thus

Believe — and sink not! doubt — and perish!
Would run the edict of the other God,
Who names me demon to his angels; they
Echo the sound to miserable things
Which knowing nought beyond their shallow senses,
Worship the word which strikes their ear, and deem

Evil or good what is proclaimed to them
In their abasement.

Kain Akt II, 2 Ende

Your reason: — let it not be over-swayed
By tyranous threats to force you into faith ...

Wie wir bereits gesehen haben zeigt sich der Einfluß
Shelley's nicht blos in der Auffassung des Gottes der Bibel
sondern auch in der Luzifer's; besonders deutlich geht dies
durch den Vergleich folgender Stellen hervor. Im „Essay
on Christianity" führt Shelley aus:

— — Milton's poem contains within itself a
philosophical refutation of that system of which, by a
strange and natural antithesis, it has been a chief popular
support. Nothing can exceed the energy and magnificence
of the character of Satan as expressed in Paradise
Lost. — — — — — — — — — — —
Milton's Devil as a moral being is as far superior
to his God. as one who perseveres in some purpose
which he has conceived to be excellent in spite of ad-
versity and torture, is to one who in the cold security
of undoubted triumph inflicts the most horrible revenge
upon his enemy.

Der zweite Teil der angeführten Stelle findet sich
außerdem in demselben Wortlaut noch in Shelley's „On the
Devil and Devils."

Auch Byron stellt Luzifer nicht blos als Geist des
Widerspruchs dar sondern er läßt ihn einen Zweck verfolgen:

Kain Akt II, 2

Lucifer: And therefore, thou canst not see if I love
Or no, except some vast and general purpose
To which particular things must melt like snows.

ferner heißt es in „On the Devils" von dem Teufel:

But is the Devil. like God, omnipresent? If so he
interpenetrates God, and they both exist coessentially:
as the metaphysicians have compared the omnipresence
of God, pervading the infinity of space and being, to
salt mixed with water.

Dieſelbe Vorſtellung findet ſich Kain Akt I Ende:

Adah.             Where dwellest thon?

Lucifer.   Throughout all space. Where should I dwell?
                                  Where are
Thy God or Gods — there am I: all things are
Divided with me; life and death — and time —
Eternity — and heaven and earth — and that
Which is not heaven nor earth — — —

Hiermit iſt die Reihe der Motive die Byron für „Kain" aus Shelley's Dichtung und Vorſtellungen erhalten hat noch nicht zu Ende. Doch kann ich auf ſie erſt in anderm Zuſammenhange zurückkommen.

Das Motiv von den beiden Prinzipen findet ſich auch in „Manfred" und auch hier wird uns ein Vergleich mit den betreffenden Stellen in Shelley's Dichtung (Queen Mab VII 199 und den andern aus „Queen Mab" und „Prometheus" angeführten Stellen) ſofort zeigen, daß Byron von ihm beinflußt wurde. Neben Ahriman dem Prinzip der Zerſtörung iſt noch ein höheres gedacht:

Manfred Akt II, 4

Bid him bow down to that which is above him,
The overruling Infinite — the Maker.

Die hier von Byron Ahriman gegebenen Attribute decken ſich mit denen die Shelley in „Queen Mab" und „Prometheus" ſeinen Perſonifikationen des böſen Prinzips giebt. So Manfred Akt II, 4

Hail to our Master — Prince of Earth and Air
Who walks the clouds and waters — in his hand
The sceptre of the elements, which tear
Themselves to chaos at his high command!
He breatheth — and a tempest shakes the sea;
He speaketh — and the clouds reply in thunder;
He gazeth — from his glance the sunbeams flee;
He moveth — earthquakes rend the world asunder.
Beneath his footsteps the volcanoes rise;
His shadow is the Pestilence; his path
The comets herald through the crackling skies;

And planets turn to ashes at his wrath
To him war offers daily sacrifice:
To him Death pays his tributes: Life is his
With all its infinite of agonies
And his the spirit of whatever is.

Eine andere Stelle aus demselben Akt Szene 3 der ebenfalls das Motiv vom bösen Prinzip zu Grunde zu liegen scheint ist:

The captive Usurper
Hurl'd down from his throne
Lay buried in torpor
Forgotten and lone.
I broke through his slumbers
I shiver'd his chain,
I leagued him with numbers —
He's Tyrant again!
With the blood of a million he'll answer my care,
With a nation's destruction — hisflight and dispair.

Diese Verse erinnern sofort an den Gang der Handlung in „Laon und Cythna". Dort wird der Tyrann von all seinen Unterthanen verlassen; dann aber kommt ihm Hülfe, und mit Feuer und Schwert wütet er nun gegen sein unglückliches Volk, das außerdem noch von Pest und Hungersnoth bedrängt wird. „Laon und Cythna" wurde zwar erst 1818 veröffentlicht, aber bereits 1817 abgefaßt, so daß hier ein Einfluß auf Byron immerhin möglich ist. Man könnte auch annehmen daß die obigen Verse mit Hinblick auf Napoleon I. gesagt sind. Mir persönlich ist es jedoch am wahrscheinlichsten, daß sie mit Hinblick auf den Kampf der beiden Prinzipe gesagt sind, in dem das Böse bald unterliegt, bald siegt. Diese Annahme scheint mir um so wahrscheinlicher, da die Geister als Diener des in Ahriman personifizierten Prinzips der Zerstörung gedacht sind. Die Vorstellung, daß Ahriman, das Prinzip der Zerstörung in der wilden Einsamkeit des Hochgebirgs hause, hat Byron ebenfalls von Shelley (vgl. Kölbing E. St. XXII S. 140). Wahrscheinlichkeit war Queen Mab VI 221, VII 84 Vorbild zu obiger Stelle.

Es kommt hier ferner noch Byron's Gedicht „Prometheus" in Betracht. Wie in Shelley's gleichnamiger dramatischer Dichtung wird in Byron's Gedicht in Juppiter das böse Prinzip personifiziert. Shelley's und Byron's Dichtung stimmen in verschiedenen Punkten überein. Da nun Shelley's Dichtung erst 1818 — 20, das Gedicht Byrons aber schon 1816 entstanden ist, so mag man geneigt sein anzunehmen daß Byron hier auf Shelley eingewirkt habe, zumal da Byron, wie wir wissen schon durch seine Schullektüre mit Äschylus „gefesselten Prometheus" bekannt geworden war, und er eine besondere Vorliebe für diesen Sagenstoff hatte; so findet sich bereits in den Hours of Idleness ein Bruchstück aus Äschylus Prometheus übersetzt. Doch ist im wesentlichen, glaube ich, das Prometheus-Motiv in der Fassung wie sie uns in Byron's Gedicht vorliegt, trotzdem aus Shelleys Dichtung gekommen. Schon in „Queen Mab" finden wir in Ahasverus das Motiv von dem unbeugsamen Gegner des tyrannischen Prinzips des Bösen, der trotz aller Leiden und Qualen in seinem Widerstand gegen dieses beharrt. In Shelley's verlorener Dichtung The Wandering Jew hat wohl der Held eine ähnliche Rolle gespielt wie Ahasverus in Queen Mab. Wir dürfen zudem wohl annehmen daß die Ahasverus-Episode in Queen Mab, ein Bruchstück aus dem Wandering Jew ist (vgl. die Anmerkung zu Queen Mab VII 67). Seine vollendeste Gestaltung hat unser Motiv dann in Shelley's Prometheus erhalten.

Zur Entstehung des Byron'schen Gedichts hat Shelley vielleicht außerdem noch dadurch beigetragen, daß er ihm während des Aufenthalts am Genfer See eine Übersetzung von Äschylus Prometheus vorlas. Die Stelle in Byron's Gedicht die meiner Meinung nach durch Shelley beeinflußt wurde lautet:

Titan! to thee the strife was given
Between the suffering and the will
Which torture where they cannot kill;
And the inexorable Heaven
And the deaf tyranny of Fate

The ruling principle of Hate
Which for its pleasure does create
The things it may annihilate
Refused the even the boon to die:
The wretched gift eternity
Was thine — and thou hast born it well.
All that the Thunderer wrung from thee
Was but the menace which flung back
On him the torments of thy rack;
The fate thou didst so well forsee
But would not to appease him tell;
And in thy Silence was his Sentence
And in his soul a vain repentance
And evil dread so ill dissembled
That in his hand the lightnings trembled.


Besonders die Übereinstimmung von Vers 11 — 20
in dem hier angeführten Passus mit dem Gang in Shelley's
Drama ist auffällig. Es finden sich sogar bei Shelley einige
Parallelstellen zu Byron's Gedicht. So

Prometheus 1 159 ff.

And at thy voice her pining sons uplifted
Their prostrate brows from the polluting dust,
And our almighty Tyrant with fierce dread
Grew pale

ibd. 371 ff.

There is a secret known
To thee, and to none else of living things,
Which may transfer the sceptre of wide Heaven,
The fear of which perplexes the Supreme.

Prometheus II, 4, 106 ff.

— — while yet his brow shook heaven, aye when
His adversary from adamantine chains
Cursed him, he trembled like a slave.

Daß Shelley hier von Byron beeinflußt wurde ist
möglich, aber zweifelhaft. Um besten wird sich die Übereinstimmung zwischen den beiden Prometheus Dichtungen

erklären laſſen, wenn wir annehmen, daß Shelley — vielleicht durch die Lektüre des gefeſſelten Prometheus angeregt —
den Plan zu ſeinem Prometheus bereits am Genfer See
faßte und wohl auch einige Stellen davon ausarbeitete. Bei
dem damaligen lebhaften Verkehr der beiden Dichter erklärt
ſich dann die Beeinfluſſung Byron's durch eine Dichtung von
der blos der Plan und einige Stellen vorhanden waren
ganz natürlich.

Im Gegenſatz zu dem Prinzip der Zerſtörung wird
die alldurchdringende, allbelebende Naturkraft als Welt-
harmonie, als Weltliebe aufgefaßt. Schon Pope ſpricht in
Essay on Man III, 1 ff. eine derartige Vorſtellung aus:

> Look round our World, behold the chain of Love
> Combining all below and all above.
> See plastic Nature working to this end,
> The single atoms each to other tend
> Attract, attracted to, the next in place
> Form'd and impell'd its neighbour to embrace.

Die Auffaſſung Shelley's von der Naturkraft als Weltliebe iſt ſo eng mit ſeiner Naturbetrachtung und ſeinem
Naturgefühl verbunden und geht ſo unmittelbar daraus
hervor, daß ich genötigt bin erſt hiervon zu ſprechen, ſelbſt
auf die Gefahr hin einigermaßen aus dem Zuſammenhang
herauszukommen.

Naturanſchauung und Naturgefühl hängen ab von
dem Verhältnis des Individuums zur Außenwelt, zum
Nicht Ich und ſeiner Auffaſſung davon. Shelley folgt
hierin Spinoza. Nach dieſem iſt das „Ich" eine Modifikation der als Intellekt aufgefaßten Subſtanz. Ähnlich ſagt
Shelley in dem Fragment „On Life":

> The words I, you, they are not signs of any actual
> difference subsisting between the assembly of thoughts
> — — — — but are merely marks employed to denote
> the different modifications of the one mind. Let it not
> be supposed that this doctrine conducts to the monstrous
> presumption that I, the person who now write and think,
> am that one mind. I am but a portion of it.

Die Ansicht daß der Einzel-Intellekt ein Teil der intellek-
tuellen Substanz ist, tritt uns auch im „Kain" entgegen:

> Thy pettier portion of the immortal part
> Of high intelligence (Kain II, l)

Es ist nicht unbedingt notwendig, hier den Einfluß
Shelley's anzunehmen, denn Byron kann diese Vorstellung
auch unmittelbar aus Spinoza geschöpft haben.

Nach Spinoza sind ferner Intellekt und Ausdehnung
vorzüglich die Attribute der Substanz. Alle Lebens- und
Daseinsformen sind Modifikationen der so gedachten Substanz
und als solche ewig. Shelley spricht dies z. B. Queen
Mab I, 273 ff. aus:

> Spirit of Nature — — — —
> Yet not the meanest worm
> That lurks in graves and fattens on the dead
> Less shares thy eternal breath.

In demselben Sinn sagt Byron „Kain" Akt. II, l

> thou
> Shalt soon return to earth and all its dust;
> Tis part of thy eternity, and mine.

Da nun das Individuum und die es umgebenden Ob-
jekte nur Modifikationen der Substanz sind, besteht zwischen
ihm und ihnen ein Gefühl der Zusammengehörigkeit und
Verwandtschaft. Auf einer unentwickelten Stufe hat der
menschliche Verstand noch nicht die Fähigkeit streng zwischen
Subjekt und Objekt zu unterscheiden. Daher der Pantheismus
der primitiven Religionen. Auch den Kindern fehlt diese
Unterscheidungsfähigkeit. So schreibt Shelley in dem Fragment
„On Life":

> We less habitually distinguished (als Kinder) all things
> that we sew and felt, from ourselves. They seemed as
> it were to constitute one mass. There are some persons
> who, in this respect, are always children. Those who
> are subject to the state called revery, feel as if their
> nature were disolved into the surrounding universe, or
> as if the surrounding universe were absorbed into their

being. And these are states which precede or accompany, or follow an unusually intense and vivid apprehension of life.

Die Leute bei denen das, was Shelley hier ausgeführt hat, der Fall ist, sind solche, die mit einem außerordentlich regen Naturgefühl begabt sind, wie er selbst und Byron. Aus diesem Naturgefühl entspringen dann ganz spontan die zahlreichen Naturbelebungen die sich in beider Dichtung finden. Donner faßt die Naturbelebungen die sich in Byron's Dichtung finden in ausgedehntem Maße als Beweise von dessen Pantheismus auf. Ich glaube, daß er hierin etwas zu weit geht, denn es finden sich schon bei diesem viele Naturbelebungen, ehe der Pantheismus ausgesprochen in seiner Dichtung auftritt.

Shelley faßt nun wie Wordsworth das Naturgefühl als ein mystisches Band zwischen der eigenen Persönlichkeit und der Außenwelt auf. In diesem Sinne haben sie dann beide wieder auf Byron gewirkt und zwar in der Weise, daß Wordsworth's Natur-Mystizismus durch Shelley vermittelt wurde teils durch dessen Dichtung, teils durch den persönlichen Verkehr. Es soll hiermit jedoch nicht gesagt sein, daß nicht einzelnes aus Wordsworth's Dichtung schon auf Byron gewirkt habe, ehe er mit Shelley bekannt wurde.

Die bedeutendsten Stellen aus Byron's Naturdichtung vor seinem Bekanntwerden mit Shelley sind wohl folgende:

C H II 25

To sit on rocks, to muse o'er flood and fell
To slowly trace the forest's shady scene
Where things that own not men's dominion dwell,
And mortal foot has never or rarely been;
To clime the trackless mountain all unseen
With the wild flock that ne'er needs a fold;
Alone over steeps and foaming falls to lean
This is not solitude, 'tis but to hold
Converse with Nature's charms and view her
       stores unrolled.

C H III 13

Where rose the mountains, there to him were friends,
Where rolled the ocean, thereon was his home,
Where a blue sky a glowing clime extends,
He had the passion and the power to roam;
The desart, forest, cavern, breaker's foam
Were unto him companionship; they spoke
A mutual language, clearer than the tome
Of his land's tongue which he would oft forsake
For Nature's pages glass'd by sunbeams on the lake.

Siege of Corinth XI

'Tis midnight, on the mountains brown
The cold brown moon shines deeply down
Blue roll the waters, blue the sky
Spreads like an ocean hung on high
Bespangled with those isles of light
So wildly spiritually bright;
Who ever gazing upon them shining
And turned to earth without repining
Nor wish'd for wings to flee away
And mix with their eternal ray?

Hier (Siege of Corinth XI) drückt alfo Byron bereits
den Wunſch aus im Univerſum aufzugehen und nicht erſt
wie Donner (S. 116) angiebt C H III 75.

Da Wordsworth's Natur-Myſtizismus auch Shelley
beeinflußt hat, will ich zunächſt einige Stellen aus ſeiner
Dichtung, in denen er ausgeſprochen wird, anführen. Die
myſtiſche Naturdichtung findet ſich außerdem, wenn ihre
Keime auch ſchon vorher vorhanden ſind, bei Shelley in
ausgedehnterem Maße erſt in den um 1816 entſtandenen
Dichtungen, wahrſcheinlich als frucht des ſchweizer Aufenthalts und der Beſchäftigung mit Wordsworth während
dieſer Zeit, ſo daß wohl deſſen Dichtkunſt hauptſächlich
Vorbild für die myſtiſche Naturdichtung Byron's wurde,
während Shelley mehr die allerdings nicht zu unterſchätzende
Rolle des Vermittlers zufiel. Aus der großen Zahl der
Stellen in denen Wordsworth's myſtiſches Naturgefühl
ausgeſprochen wird, will ich die folgenden anführen:

Lines, composed, above Tintern Abbey 71 ff. (1798):

For nature then

\*    \*    \*

To me was all in all — — -- — — —
— — — — The sounding chatatact
Haunted me like a passion: the tall rock,
The mountain, and the deep and gloomy wood,
Their colours and their forms, were then to me
An appetite; a feeling and a love

Ebenda 35 ff.

Nor less, I trust,
To them I may have owed another gift,
Of aspect more sublime; that blessed mood,
In which the burthen of the mystery,
In which the heavy and the weary weight
Of all this unintelligieble world,
Is lightoned: that serene and blessed mood,
In which the affections gently lead us on, —
Until, the breath of this corporeal frame
And even the motion of our human blood
Almost suspended, we are laid asleep
In body, and become a living soul:
While with an eye made quiet by the power
Of harmony, and the deep power of joy,
We see into the life of things.

Excursion I, 205 ff.

Sound needed none,
Nor any voice of joy: his spirit drank
The spectacle: sensation, soul and form,
All melted into him: they swallowed up
His animal being: in them did he live,
And by them did he live, they were his life.
In such access of mind, in such high hour
Of visitation from the living God
Thought was not: in enjoyment it expired;

*     *     *

223 ff.                                 Early had he learned
To reverence the volume that displays
The mystery, the life which cannot die:
But in the mountains did he feel his faith,
All things, responsive to the writing. there
Breathed immortality, revolving life,
And greatness still revolving; infinite:
There littleness was not; the least of things
Seemed infinite.

Ferner Excursion I, 241 ff. 263, 185 ff. 203 ff. 280 ff.

Stellen in denen Shelley sein mystisches Naturgefühl
zum Ausdruck bringt sind:

Queen Mab IV 6 ff.

> Yon gentle hills,
> — — — — — — —
> — — — — — — — — yon castled steep
> — — — — — — — —
> — — — — — — — All form a scene
> Where musing solitude might love to lift
> Her soul above this sphere of earthliness.

Alastor 651.

> The poets blood which ever beat
> In mystic sympathy with Nature's ebb and flow.

Mont Blanc II, 34 ff.

> Dizzy Ravine! and when I gaze on thee
> I seem as in a trance sublime and strange
> To muse on my own seperate phantasy,
> My own, my human mind, which passively,
> Now renders and receives fast influencings
> Holding an unremitting interchange
> With the clear universe of things around.

Fragment „On Love":

> Thou demandest what is Love. It is that powerful
> attraction towards all we conceive, or, fear, or hope
> beyond ourselves when we — — — — seek to awaken in
> all things that are, a community with what we experience
> within ourselves — — — This is love. It is the bond
> and the sanction which connects not only man with
> man, but wirth every thing which exists.

Wordsworth und Shelley gehn sogar soweit dieses
mystische Naturgefühl als Liebe aufzufassen.

So sagt Wordsworth:

Excursion I 241

> To look on Nature with a humble heart
> Selfquestioned where it did not understand,
> And with a superstitious eye of love.

Daß Shelley das myftifche Naturgefühl als Liebe auffaßt geht aus der bereits angeführten Stelle aus „On Love" hervor.

Von diesem myftifchen Naturgefühl Shelley's und Wordsworth's zeigt fich Byron befonders in C H III beeinflußt. So in

C H III, 72

I live not in myself, but I become
Portion of that around me and to me
High mountains are a feeling.

C H III, 75

Are not the mountains, waves and skies a part
Of me and of my soul, as I of them
Is not the love of these deep in my heart
With a pure passion? — — — —

C H III, 88

Ye stars — — — — —
— — — — — — — — —
— — — 'tis to be for given
That in our aspirations to be great
Our destinies o'erleap their mortal state
And claim a kindred with you — — —

Überhaupt ift das myftifch gefteigerte Naturgefühl der Grundton im ganzen zweiten Teil von C H III.

Daß die myftifche Naturbetrachtung zu jener Zeit bei ihm im Vordergrund ftand, fpricht Byron felbft im Dream VIII aus:

— — — with the stars
And the quick Spirit of the Universe
He held his dialogues and they did teach
To him the magic of their mysteries.
To him the book of Night was opened wide,
And voices from the abyss revealed
A marvel and a secret.

Dieses mystische Naturgefühl findet sich ferner noch
ausgesprochen in „Monody on the Death of Sheridan":

When the last sunshine of expiring day
In summer's twylight weeps itself away,
Who has not felt the softness of the hour?
Sink on the heart, as dew along the flower?
With a pure feeling which absorbs and awes,
While Nature makes that melancholy pause,
Her breathing moment on the bridge, where Time
Of light and darkness forms an arch sublime,
Who hath not shared that calm so still and deep,
The voiceless thought which would not speak
        but weep,
A holy concord — and a bright regret,
A glorious sympathy with suns that set?

Wie Byron selbst zugab, ist er hier im Ausdruck des
Naturgefühls Wordsworth gefolgt. Als Vorbild hat ihm
wohl folgendes aus dessen Dichtung vorgeschwebt:

Calm is all nature as a resting wheel
The kine are couched upon the dewy grass;
— — — — — — — —
Dark is the ground a slumber seems to steal
O'er vale, and mountain, and the starless sky.
Now in this blank of things, a harmony,
Home-felt and home-created, comes to heal
That grief for which the senses still supply
Fresh food; for only then, when, memory
Is hushed, I am at rest.

Dem, der wie Wordsworth und Shelley sich mit der
Natur im Einklang fühlt, erscheint diese selbst als eine
gewaltige Harmonie. So sagt Shelley im Anschluß aus der
bereits angeführten Stelle aus „On Love":

Hence in solitude — — — we love the flowers,
the grass, the waters, and the sky. In the motion of the
very leaves of spring, in the blue air, there is then
found a secret correspondence with our heart. There
is eloquence in the tongueless wind, and a melody in
the flowing brooks and the rustling of the reets beside
them which by their inconceivable relation, to something

within the soul, awaken the spirit to a dance of breath-
les rapture, and bring tears of mysterious tenderness to
the eyes — — — — Sterne says if he were in a
desart he would love some cypress.

Die Harmonie der Natur ist eine von den Lieblings-
ideen Shelley's. So spricht er Queen Mab II 257 von:
Nature's unchanging harmony und in Brief IV der letters
written during a residence in the environs of Geneva
sagt er: Nature was the poet, whose harmony held our
spirit more breathless than that of the divinest. Ferner
Queen Mab I, 52

> — — that strange lyre whose strings
> The genii of the breezes swéep.

Zum Teil war hier erst wohl Wordsworth wieder
Vorgänger und Vorbild für Shelley. Er sagt z. B.

Excursion II 696 ff.

> Many are the notes
> Which in his tuneful course, the wind draws forth
> From rocks, woods, caverns, heaths and dashing
> > > shores

> — — — — — — — —
> — — — — Nor have nature's laws
> Left them ungifted with a power to yield
> Music of finer tone: a harmony,
> So do I call it — — —
> — — though there be no voice, the clouds
> The mist, the shadows, light of golden suns
> Motions of moonlight, all thither — touch
> And have an answer, thither come and shape
> A language — — — —

Der Einfluß Wordsworth's und Shelley's in dieser
Hinsicht tritt in folgenden Stellen aus Byron's Dichtung
zu Tage.

C H III 90

> Then stirs the feeling infinite so felt
> In solitude, where we are least alone
> A truth which through our being then doth melt
> And purifies from self: it is a tone

The soul and source of music which makes known
Eternel harmony, and sheds a charm,
Like to the fabled Cytherea's zone
Binding all things with beauty.

Island XVIII

No dying night breeze, harping o'er the hill,
Striking the strings of nature, rock and tree
Those best and earliest lyres of harmony —

Don Iuan XV, 5

There's music in the sighing of a reed;
There's music in the gushing of a rill;
There's music in all things, if men had ears
Their earth is but an echo of the spheres.

(Vgl. die angeführte Stelle aus on Love)

Die Harmonie der Natur wird jedoch durch den Menschen
geftört:

Queen Mab VII, 195

              All things speak
Peace, harmony, and love. The universe
In nature's silent eloquence declares
That all fulfill  the works of love and joy,
All but outcast man.

Denselben Gedanken drückt Byron in Manfred I,2 aus:

How beautiful is all this visible world
How glorious in its action and itself
But we —  —  —  —
— — — — — make
A conflict of its elements.

Ebenso in C H IV 126:

Our life is a false nature — 'tis not in
The harmony of things.

Wie aus dem vorausgegangenen erfichtlich ift, faffen
Wordsworth und Shelley die Natur als Harmonie auf.
Es folgt daraus, daß die fchaffende Naturkraft felbft Harmonie,
die höchfte Harmonie — Liebe fein muß. Wir kommen
fo zu der Auffaffung des Weltgefeßes als Liebe. Ich habe

bereits darauf hingewiesen, daß Pope in Essay on Man III
eine ähnliche Auffassung hat. Die Grundlage zu · der Auf=
faffung Wordsworth's und Shelley's von dem Weltgesetz,
von der Substanz als Liebe ist teilweise bei Spinoza zu
finden.

Bei Spinoza ist die Liebe zur Natur die zur Liebe
gesteigerte Resignation in die Notwendigkeit des Weltgesetzes
(·Subftanz). Diese Liebe (amor intellectualis Dei) zu Sub=
stanz, (Natur, Gott) wird für den Menschen die Quelle
ewigen Glücks. Durch dieses eigenartige Gefühl wird der
Unterschied zwischen Substanz und Modifikation (Individuum)
aufgehoben. Der amor intellectualis Dei des Menschen
wird bei Spinoza identisch mit der Liebe Gottes zu sich
selbst, und die menschliche Seele die vergänglich ist in ihrer
an den Körper gebundenen Erscheinung wird dadurch un=
sterblich (vergl. Spinoza Tractatus politicus I, 4, Ethik 17, 21,
32, 34, 36).

Bei Shelley und Wordsworth jedoch geht das Gefühl
der Liebe zur Natur nicht sowohl aus der Resignation in
die Weltnotwendigkeit, als aus dem durch das Gefühl der
Wesensverwandschaft hervorgerufenen Einklang, der Sym=
pathie des Menschen mit der Natur hervor. Diese Liebe erhebt
dann wieder wie bei Spinoza — besonders nach Shelley's
Auffassung — den Menschen über die Schranken des
Irdischen. Durch die „Transformation der Naturen" wird
dann die Naturkraft — das Weltgesetz selbst die Liebe.

Da auch hier Wordsworth der Vorgänger und zum
Teil das Vorbild für Shelley war, will ich zuerst einige
Stellen aus seiner Dichtung anführen aus denen diese Auf=
faffung hervorgeht:

To my sister (1798)
Love, now a universal birth
From heart to heart is stealing
From earth to man, from man to earth
— — — — — — — — —
— — — — — — — — —
It is the hour of feeling.

And from the blessed power that rolls
About, below, above
We'll frame the measure of our souls
They shall be tuned to love.

## Heart Leap Well 165 ff. (1800)

The being that is in the clouds and air
That is in the green leaves among the groves
Maintains a deep and reverential care for
The the unoffending creatures whom he loves.

## Excursion IV 427

These craggy regions, these chaotic wilds
Does that benignity pervade, that warms
The mole — — — —

## Excursion IV 1208

For, the Man
Who communes with the Forms
Of Nature — — — — — —
— — — — — — needs must feel
The joy of that pure principle of love.

## Excursion V 1002

— — — life is love and immortality,
The being one, and one the element.

## ibd. 1012

Life is energy of love.

## Tribute to the memoy of the same dog (1805)

For love that comes wherever life and sense
Are given by God, in thee was most intense;
A chain of heart, a feeling of the mind,
A tender sympathy, which did thee bind
Not only to us Men, but to thy Kind;
Yea for thy fellow-brutes in thee we saw
A soul of love, love's intellectual law.


Bei Shelley findet sich die Auffassung, daß Liebe und
Natur, Substanz ein und dasselbe sind, erst verhältnismäßig
spät, obwohl gerade das Motiv von der myftischen, pantheistischen Liebe eine sehr große Rolle in seiner Dichtung
spielt. Die Zahl der hierfür in Betracht kommenden Stellen
ist sehr groß. Von den wichtigern seien folgende aus-
gewählt.

Prometheus II Sc. 5, 25 ff.

Love, like the atmosphere
Of the sun's fire filling the living world

— — — — — — — —

Hear'st thou not the sounds i' the air which
speak the love
Of all articulate beings?

Sensitive Plant XXV

And, when evening descended from heaven above
And the earth was all rest and the air was
all love.

Epipsychidion 475 ff.

Till the isle's beauty, like a naked bride
Glowing at once with love and loveliness,
Blushes and trembles at its own excess:
Yet like a buried Lamp, a Soul no less
Burns in the heart of this delicious isle,
An atom of the Eternal, whose own smile
Unfolds itself, and may be felt not seen
O' er the gray rocks, blue waves, and forests
green,
Filling their bare and void interstices.

Prometheus II 215 Sc. 5, 95 ff.

Realms where the air we breathe is love,
Which in the winds and in the waves doth move,
Harmonizing this earth with what we feel above.

Ode to Naples

Great spirit, deepest Love
Which rulest and dost move
All things which live and are.

Vgl. ferner noch hierzu „Prince Athanese" 134 ff.
Adonais 42, 54. With a Guitar to Jane („The woods
were in their winter sleep" ff).

Es geht aus einem Vergleich dieser Stellen mit denen
aus Wordsworth hervor, daß Shelley das Motiv von der
pantheistischen Liebe wohl von diesem hat, daß er es aber
selbständig umgestaltet und weitergebildet hat. In Shelley's

Dichtung hat wie gesagt, dieses Motiv erst in verhältnismäßig später Zeit in ausgedehntem Maße Verwendung
gefunden.

In C. H. III 99 ff bringt nun Byron der Liebe als
Weltprinzip einen Hymnus dar. Es wurde schon oft darauf
hingewiesen, daß er hier von Shelley beeinflußt worden ist.
Obgleich wir in dessen Dichtung erst in den angeführten
Stellen aus Prometheus seine mystisch-pantheistische Auf-
fassung von der Liebe als Weltprinzip in so klassischer
Weise zum Ausdruck gebracht finden, wie es Byron in
C. H III 99 ff gethan hat, so sind die betreffenden Stanzen
doch so durchtränkt mit Shelley's mystischem Naturgefühl und
Liebesmystizismus, daß man seinen Einfluß sofort erkennt,
Ja ich glaube behaupten zu können, daß wenn von C H III
nichts weiter bekannt wäre als Stanze 99—102 und der
Name des Verfassers unbekannt, man sie unbedenklich
Shelley zuschreiben würde. Die mystisch-pantheistische Auffassung von der Liebe, die hier zu Tage tritt, ist himmel-
weit verschieden von Byron's sonst im allgemeinen sehr
realistischer Auffassung davon. Inwieweit sein Verhältnis
zu Miß Clairmont diesen Liebes-Enthusiasmus beeinflußt
hat, mag dahingestellt bleiben. Neben Shelley mag auch
einzelnes aus Wordsworth mitgewirkt haben, doch scheint
mir dessen Einfluß hier erst an zweiter Stelle zu kommen.
Die betreffenden Stanzen aus C. H. III lauten:

## XCIX.

Carens! sweet Clarens, birthplace of deep Love
Thine air is the young breath of passionate thought,
Thy trees take root in Love; the snows above
The very glaciers have his colours caught,
And sunset into rose-hues sees them wrought,
By rays which sleep there lovingly: the rocks
The permanent cracks, tell here of Love, who
                        sought
In them a refuge from the wordly shocks
Which stir and sting the soul with hope that
                        wooes then mocks.

## C.

Clarence by heavenly feet thy paths are trod, —
Undying Love's, who here ascends a throne
To which the steps are mountains, where the god
Is a pervading life and light, so shown
Not on these summits solely, nor alone
In the still cave and forest; o'er the flower
His eye is sparkling, and his breath has blown,
His soft and summer breath, whose tender power
Passes the strength of storms in their most
desolate hour.

## CI.

All things are here of him; from the black pines
Which are his shade on high, and the loud roar
Of torrents, where he listens, to the vines
Which slope his green path downward to the
shore,
Where the bow'd waters meet him and adore,
Kissing his feet with murmurs; and the wood,
The covert of old trees, with trunks all hoar,
But light leaves, young as joy, stands where it stood
Offering to him and his, a populous solitude.

## CII.

A populous solitude of bees and birds
And fairy-formed and many — coloured things,
Who worship with notes more sweet than words,
And innocently open their glad wings,
Fearless and full of life: the gush of springs
And fall of lofty fountains, and the bend
Of stirring branches and the but which brings
The swiftest thought of beauty, here extend
Mingling and made by Love unto one mighty end.

Der Zweckgedanke der im letzten Vers ausgesprochen
wird, ist Byron sonst fremd (vergl. Donner S. 113). Shelley
nimmt bald einen Zweck in der schaffenden Natur an, bald
läugnet er ihn. Als zweckmäßig schaffend wird die Natur
bei ihm z. B. am Ende von Queen Mab gedacht und in

4

Epipsychidion 360 sagt er gleichfalls, daß ihr Schaffen zielt:
to one sweet end
was eine Parallele zu dem obigen unto one migthy end
ist. Vielleicht ist also der hier ausgesprochene Zweckgedanke
auf Shelley's Einfluß zurückzuführen.

In der Anmerkung zu Stanze 100 giebt dann Byron
selbst eine kurze Darstellung von der pantheistischen Liebes-
philosophie Shelley's.

Er sagt hier:

— — — — But this is not all: the feeling with
which all around Clarens, and the opposite rocks of
Meillerie are invested is of a still higher and more com-
prehensive order than the mere sympathy with individual
passion; it is a sense of the existence of love in its
most extended and sublime capacity, and of our own
participation of its good and its glory; it is the great
principle of the universe, which is there more condensed,
but not less manifested; and of which though knowing
ourselves a part we loose our individuality and mingle in
the beauty of the whole.

Diese pantheistische Liebesschwärmerei ist jedoch bei
Byron nur vorübergehend. Sie findet sich nur hier und
Nachklänge davon vielleicht in Lament of Tasso VI:

It is no marvel — from my very birth
My soul was drunk with love — which did pervade
And mingle with whate'er I saw on earth.

und in einzelnen Stellen in „The Island" und „Heaven and
Earth". Hier tritt jedoch weniger die Auffassung von der
Liebe als Weltprinzip hervor, als die, daß wir durch sie
über die Schranken der Persönlichkeit hinweg gesetzt und
mit der Gottheit vereinigt werden. Auch dieser Vorstellung
begegnen wir öfters bei Shelley, und Byron hat sie wohl
von ihm. So sagt Shelley Prometheus II 5, 40.

Common as light is love
— — — — — — — —
It makes the reptile equal to the god

Epipſychidion 128

the spirit
Of the worm beneath the sod
In love and worship blends itself with god.

Daß Byron dieſe Ideen Shelley's recht gut kannte, geht aus einer Anſpielung desſelben auf dieſe Stelle in ſeinem Sonnet „to Byron" hervor.

Ferner ſagt er in dieſem Sinne:
Prometheus II
Fate, Time, Occasion, Chance and Change? To these,
All things are subject but eternal Love.
Arethusa V
When they love, but live no more.

Andere Stellen, in denen dieſe Auffaſſung ſich findet, ſind Zastrozzi paſſim, in dem Gedicht Love, Fragment Wealth and dominion (1817), Prometheus IV paſſim, Sensitive Plant, Conclusion VI.

Dieſe Vorſtellung Shelley's von der Liebe findet ſich bei Byron:

Heaven and Earth Scene 1.
Thine immortality cannot repay
With love more warm than mine
My love. There is a ray
In me, which. — — — — —
I feel was lighted at thy God's and thine.

Ferner Island XVI.
Dieſe Stelle zeigt wieder eine Verknüpfung von Liebe⸗ und Naturgefühl, erinnert ſomit an C. H. III, da ich einen Teil davon bereits vorher angeführt habe, ſo beſchränke ich mich darauf, blos den Anfang hier zu bringen, der noch anderweitig für den Einfluß Shelley's in Betracht kommt:

— — — — — — the devotee
Lives not on earth, but in his ecstasy
Around him days and worlds are heedless driven,
His soul is gone before his dust to heaven.

Is love less potent? No -- his path is trod,
Alike uplifted gloriously to God;
Or link'd to all we know of heaven below
— — — — — — — —
— — — — — the all absorbing flame
Which kindled by another grows the same
Wrapt in one blaze; the pure, yet funeral pile
Where gentle hearts, like Brahmins, sit and
smile.

Bei der Stelle Alike uplifted — heaven below
hat Byron vielleicht die folgende aus Scott's Lay of the last
Minstrel III, 2 vorgeschwebt:

Heaven is love and love is heaven.

Es wird am Ende unserer Stelle aus „Island" XVI
außerdem noch die Liebe mit dem Tode verglichen.

Eine Parallele hierzu ist:

Island VI

— —· — — passion's desolating joy
Too powerful over every heart, but most
O'er those who burning in the new born fire
Like martyrs revel in their funeral pyre,
With such devotion to their ecstasy
That life knows no such rapture as to die:
And die they do, for earthly life has nought
Match'd with that burst of Nature, even in thought
And all our dreams of better life above
But close in one eternal gush of love.

Diese Vorstellung, daß die Liebe uns unvergängliches
Leben giebt, uns der Sphäre des irdischen Daseins enträckt,
geht wohl wieder auf Shelley zurück. Dieser sagt in solchem
Sinne z. B.:

Rosalind and Helen 1123 ff.

Heardst thou not, that those who die
Awake in a world of ecstasy;
That love, when limbs are interwoven,

And sleep, when the night of life is cloven,
And thought, to the worlds dim boundaries
clinging,
And music when one beloved is singing,
Is death?

Epipsychidion 169 ff.

Narrow
The heart that loves, the brain that contemplates,
The life that wears, the spirit that creates
One object, and one form, and builds thereby
A sepulchre for its eternity.

Aus den Worten „And thought, to the worlds dim
boundaries clinging" in der angeführten Stelle aus Rosalind und Helen geht hervor, daß nach Shelley's Auffassung
nicht blos die Liebe, sondern auch die Naturbetrachtung den
Menschen über die Schranken des Jrdischen erhebt. Jn
diesem Sinne sagt er noch:

Marenghi XXIII (1818)
And in the moonless nights, when the dim ocean
Heaved underneath the heaven, — — —
Starting from dreams
Communed with the immeasurable world;
And felt his life beyond his limbs dilated,
Till his mind grew like that it contemplated.

Von dieser Vorstellung ist wohl Byron in Island XVI
beeinflußt, wenn er sagt:

Are the waves
Without a spirit? Are the dropping caves
Without a feeling in their silent tears?
No no; — they woo and clasp us to their spheres
Dissolve this clog and clod of clay before
Its hour, and merge our souls in the great shore,
Strip off this fond and false identity! —

Diese Stelle steht in engstem Zusammenhang mit
Byron's bereits besprochenem Wunsch im Universum aufzugehn.

Jm vorausgehenden haben wir gesehen, wie Shelley's
Auffassung von Substanz, Gott, Natur, Byron beeinflußt

hat, oder sagen wir vielmehr dessen Dichtung; denn ich will natürlich nicht behaupten, daß Byron erst durch Shelley zum Teil ganz gewöhnliche philosophische Ideen und Vorstellungen kennen gelernt habe; wohl aber hat er durch ihn gelernt sie als Motive in seiner Dichtung zu verwerten. Im folgenden soll es jetzt meine Aufgabe sein zu untersuchen, wie Shelley's Auffassung von der Modifikation der Substanz, dem Individuum, seine Vorstellungen von Leben und Tod auf Byron's Dichtung befruchtend gewirkt haben.

Nach Spinoza entstehen die individuellen Lebens- und Daseinsformen durch die Modifikationen der Substanz. Diese Modifikationen werden durch Bewegung verursacht. Unendlich und ewig wie die Substanz ist auch die Bewegung und unendlich sind die durch die Bewegung hervorgerufenen Daseinserscheinungen.

In diesem Sinne sagt Shelley z. B.

Queen Mab VI 162.

— — the restless wheals of being
Whose flashing spokes, instinct with infinite life
Bicker and burn — — —

Queen Mab IV.

boundless realm of unending change

In dem Gedicht Mutability

Nought may endure but Mutability.

Die Vorstellung von der Unendlichkeit des Lebens und Seins findet sich auch bei Wordsworth. So:

Excursion IV 9

abyss
Of infinite Being.

Byron könnte diese Vorstellungen, wie so manche andere, die bereits behandelt sind, direkt aus Spinoza haben. Dagegen spricht jedoch, daß sie sich in seiner Dichtung erst nach seinem Bekanntwerden mit Shelley finden, während er Spinoza bereits geraume Zeit vorher kannte. Wir werden deshalb immerhin Shelley's Einfluß annehmen dürfen, wo er von der Unendlichkeit des Seins und des Wechsels spricht, wie in folgenden Stellen:

Island II.
>     The eternal change
>     But grasps humanity with quicker range.

Kain II, 1.
>     — — — moments only and the space
>     Have been and must be all unchangeable

Kain II, 2
>     Infinity of life

ibd.
>                         the immensity
>     Of worlds and hife.

Da der Wechsel seit ewigen Zeiten stattfindet, so liegt der Gedanke nahe, daß alles, was uns jetzt unbelebt erscheint, einmal belebt war. Diesen Gedanken hat Shelley in seiner Dichtung öfter ausgesprochen. So:

Queen Mab V 212.
>     There's not one atom of yon earth
>     But once was living man

Letter to Maria Gisborne (vgl. Kölbing, Byron-Ausgabe B 2 S. 407)
>     This world would smell like what it is — a tomb:

Zurück geht diese düstere Vorstellung wahrscheinlich auf Taylor, ‚Holy dying l. 1:
>     — — — — and you can go nowhither, but you tread upon a dead man's bones.

Dieser düstere Gedanke scheint Byron's melancholischem Gemüt besonders zugesagt zu haben; er kommt mehrmals auf ihn zurück. So:

Churchills Grave (1816)
>     Earth is but a tombstone
>
>     Could I remount
>     The ashes of a thousand ages spread
>     Wherever man has trodden or shall tread.

Sardanapalus IV, 1
>     The dust we tread upon was once alive
>     And wretched.

Wie wir gesehen haben teilt Shelley die Ansicht Spinoza's, daß die einzelnen Daseinsformen Modifikationen der Subftanz find. Durch die Modififation der als Jntellekt aufgefaßten Subftanz erhalten wir den Einzel Jntellekt. Der menfchliche Geift fühlt fich nun in feiner an den Körper gebundenen Geftalt befchränkt und gefeffelt. So heißt es:

Queen Mab VI 190 ff.

Soul of the Universe! eternal spring
Of life and death, of happiness and woe
Of all that chequers the phantasmal scene
That floats before our eyes in wavering light,
Which gleams but on the darkness of our prison
Whose chains and massy walls
We feel, but cannot see.

Jn diefem Sinne fpricht Byron C. H III 73 von:

— — claycold bonds which round our being cling.

Der Wunfch, fich von den Schranken des irdifchen Dafeins befreit zu fehen wird, wie wir gefehen haben, fchon in Siege of Corinth XI von ihm ausgefprochen. Er braucht alfo hier nicht von Shelley beeinflußt zu fein. Daß jedoch Gegenftände wie der vorliegende, in den Bereich ihrer Unter-haltung gehört haben geht aus Julian und Maddalo hervor:

And such — is our mortality ff.

Die als Jntellekt aufgefaßte Subftanz ift ohne Bewußt-fein. Diefes findet fich erft in dem durch ihre Modififation entftehenden Einzel-Jntellekt:

Queen Mab IX 155 ff.

For birth but wakes the spirit to the sense
Of outward shows — — — —

Von diefer Vorftellung zeigt fich Byron beeinflußt Kain II, 2:

                                innumerable
Yet unborn myriads of unconscious atoms
All to be animated — — — — —

Nach dem Tode vereinigt fich die Modifikation wieder mit der Subftanz. Hier ift Shelley zum Teil wieder Nach-folger und Nachahmer von Wordsworth. So in dem Gedicht To William Shelley (1819).

Where art thou, my gentle child?
Let me think thy spirit feeds,
With its life intense and mild,
The love of loving leaves and weeds
Among these tombs and ruins wild; —
Let me think that, through low seeds
Of the sweet flowers and sunny grass,
Into their hues and scents may pass
A portion — — — — — —

Adonais XLII

He is made one with Nature. There is heard
His voice in all her music, from the moan
Of thunder to the song of night's sweet bird.
He is a presenc to be felt and known
In darkness and in light, from herb and stone,
Spreading itself where'er that Power may move
Which wields the world with never-wearied love
Sustains it from beneath, and kindles it above.


Das Vorbild zu diesen Stellen ist in einem von
Wordsworth's Lucy-Liedern zu finden:

Three years she grew in sun and shower,
Then Nature said, „A lovelier flower
On earth was never sown.
This child I to myself will take
She shall be mine, and I will make
A Lady of my own.

Myself will to my darling be
Both law and impulse; and with me
The girl, in rock and plain,
In earth and heaven, in glade and bower
Shall feel an overseeing power
To kindle or restrain".


Die hier vom Tod ausgesprochene Auffassung findet
sich bei Shelley noch in „An address to the people on the
death of the princess Charlotte": in den Worten When
that Power through which we live ceases to maintain the
life which it has conferred — — — —

Der Einfluß Shelley's und Wordsworth's auf Byron in dieser Hinsicht zeigt sich an folgenden Stellen:

C H IV 151. Byron sagt hier von der jungen Römerin die im Gefängnis ihren greisen Vater mit der eigenen Milch ernährt:

Oh, holiest nurse!
No drop of that clear stream its way shall miss
To thy sire's heart, replenishing its source
With life, as our freed souls rejoin the universe.

Don Juan III 104                    [Whole
Earth, air, stars, all that springs from the great
Who has produced and will receive the soul.

Wenn nun der Einzel-Intellekt, die Seele nach dem Tode wieder mit der Substanz vereinigt wird, so kann zweierlei eintreten: Das Bewußtsein, das erst durch die Modifikation entstanden ist, schwindet wieder, oder aber die von ihren Fesseln befreite Seele erwacht in der Vereinigung mit der Substanz, dem Quell alles Lebens zu neuem, höherem Dasein. In diesem Sinne sagt Wordsworth Excursion III 690 ff.

— — — — to the grave I spake
Imploringly; looked up, and asked the Heavens
If Angels traversed their cerulean floors,
If fixed or wandering star could tidings yield
Of the departed spirit — what abode
It occupies — what consciousness retains
Of former loves and interests.

Shelley nimmt bald an, daß mit dem Tod alles aus ist, bald das Gegenteil. In dem Fragment On the punishment of death sagt er z. B.

— — — the vital principle within us, in whatwer mode it may continue to exist, must loose that consciousnous of definite and individual being which characterizes it, and become a unit in the vast sum of action and of thought which disposes and animates the universe, and is called God — — — —

Auf der andern Seite sagt er jedoch:

(Love 1811)
    Each energy of soul surviving
    More vivid soars above
Ähnlich in Adonais
    Peace, peace he is not dead
    He is awaken'd from the dream of life
Byron teilt dieses Schwanken Shelley's. So sagt er
Manfred III 3,:
    The mind which is immortal makes itself
    Requital for its good or evil thoughts,
    Is its own origin of ill and end
    And its own place and time — its innate sense
    When stripped of this mortality, derives
    No colour from the fleeting things without;
Dagegen C H III 74:
    And when at length, the mind shall be all free
    From what it hates in this degraded form,
    Reft of its carnal life, safe what shall be
    Existent happier in the fly and worm,
    When elements to elements conform,
    And dust is as it should be, shall I not
    Feel all I see less dazzling, but more warm?
    The bodiless thought? the Spirit of each spot?
    Of which, even now, I share at times the
                                immortal lot.
Dieselbe Ansicht findet sich „Kain" II 2:
                Be content; it will
    Seem clearer to thine immortality.

Daß alles als Teil der unvergänglichen Substanz
unvergänglich ist spricht Shelley aus:
    Epipsychidion, Cancelled passages of that poem:
        — — — — the immortality
    Of this great world, which all things must
    Adonais XX:                          inherit
                Nought we know dies.

Die gleiche Vorstellung liegt zu Grunde wenn Byron sagt:
Kain II. 1

Lucifer.                    On then, with me
    Wouldst thou behold things mortal or immortal?
Cain, Why, what are things?

Lucifer                    Both partly
Heaven and earth Scene 1:
I feel my immortality o'ersweep
All pains, all tears, all time, all fears and peal,
Like the eternal thunders of the deep,
Into my ears this truth — Thou liv'st for ever!
But if it be in joy
I know not, nor would know,
That secret rests with the Almighty giver
Who folds in clouds the fonts of bliss and woe
But thee and me he never can destroy;
Change us he may, but not o'erwhelm; we are
Of as eternal essence.

Der Tod ift nach diefer Auffaffung alfo kein Ende
fondern blos ein Wechfel. So fagt Shelley u. a. in dem
fragment „Death":

— — that mystery death is a change.

ferner Hellas 34: Life may change but it may fly not.
und in gleicher Weife Byron im Kain II, 1:

But changes make noth death, except to clay.

Es ergiebt fich aus dem vorhergehenden, da der Tod
blos 'ein Wandel ift, daß er nichts wirkliches ift. Da die
Seele in der Vereinigung mit der Subftanz zu höherem
Dafein erwacht, fo kann man das Leben als einen Zuftand
auffaffen, in dem nicht alle feelifchen Kräfte frei walten —
als einen Traum. So fagt Shelley:

Adonais
Peace, peace, he is not dead, he doth not sleep,
He hath awaken'd from the dream of life.

Shelley ftellt fogar die paradoxe Behauptung auf:
we are death (fragment „Death 1820"). Auf der andern
Seite fagt er ebenfo paradox von der Nichtwirklichkeit des
Todes: 'Tis Death is dead (Adonais XLI.) Byron fpricht
von der Unwirklichkeit des Todes C H III 30:

— — — 'twould disarm
The spectre Death, had he substantial power to harm

Diefe Stelle ift zwar früher als die aus Shelley
angeführten aber deffen Einfluß ift hier doch möglich, da

die Vorstellung von der Unwirklichkeit des Todes bei ihm
ein häufiges Motiv ist während sie bei Byron meines
Wissens nur hier vorkommt.

Jn diesen Zusammenhang gehört auch eine Stelle
die in ziemlich dunkler Weise über den Tod spricht und die
meiner Meinung nach von Donner nicht richtig aufgefaßt
wurde (vgl. Donner S. 124). Sie findet sich in „Could
I remount the river of my years":

Wat is this Death? — a quiet of the heart
The whole of that, of which we are a part?
For life is but a vision — what I see
Of all which lives alone is life to me,
And being so — the absent are the dead.
— — — — — — —
The absent are the dead — for they are cold,
And never can be what once we did behold;
And they are changed, and cheerless, — or
                                    if yet
The unforgotten do not all forget,
Since thus divided — equal must it be
If the deep barrier be of earth or sea;
It may be both — but one day end it must
In the dark union of insensate dust.
The under-earth inhabitants are they
But mingled millions decomposed to clay?
— — — — — — —
Or do they in their silent cities dwell
Each in his incommunicative cell?
Or have they their own language? and a sense
Of breathless being? — darken'd and intense
As midnight in her solitude?

Was die Erklärung der ersten beiden Zeilen anbelangt
so liegt diese wohl auf der Hand. Das Jndividuum ist eine
Modifikation der Substanz — ein Teil von ihr. Durch den
Tod wird die Modifikation, der Teil, wieder mit der
Substanz, dem großen Ganzen, vereinigt. Tod ist hier
prägnant - Zustand in dem Tod gebraucht; daher

      ... — — Death — — — — — —
      The whole of that of which we are a part.

Die Erklärung der Worte „For Life is but a vision"
liegt ebenfalls auf der Hand. Da die Substanz selbst
unveränderlich ist, ist das Leben mit all seinen wechselnden
Erscheinungen nichts wirkliches, reales — but a vision.
Diese Vorstellung findet sich sehr oft bei Shelley.
Schon in Queen Mab spricht er von „fleeting scene of things".

Ferner sagt er in Hellas 407

— this Whole of
Of suns and worlds and men and beasts and
                                      flowers
— — — — ... — — — ...
Is but a vision.

In Letter to Maria Gisborne
— — this familiar life, which seems to be
But is not — — — —

In gleichem Sinne sagt Byron später noch einmal in
„Don Juan" VII 3:
What after all, are all things but a show.

Man könnte zwar die Worte For life is but a vision
auch noch anders erklären, indem man sie mit dem folgenden
in Zusammenhang bringt. Hier sagt Byron:
— what I see
Of all which lives alone is life to me.

Also nur was gesehen wird — wahrgenommen wird
ist Leben — existiert. Daher:
life is but a vision.

Byron spricht hier eine philosophische Idee aus, die
ihm bis dahin fremd gewesen war oder wenigstens noch
nicht in seiner Dichtung ausgesprochen wurde.
Der Satz, daß blos das, was wahrgenommen wird
existiert ist der Fundamental-Satz der spiritualistischen Philosophie Berkeley's. Dieser lehrt: Existenz, Leben beruht auf
dem Vermögen wahrgenommen zu werden oder wahrzunehmen.
Was nicht wahrgenommen werden kann oder nicht wahrnimmt
existiert nicht. Die Existenz eines Objects kann nicht ohne

wahrnehmendes Subjekt gedacht werden. Shelley hat sich mit der Philosophie Berkeley's sehr eingehend beschäftigt. So schreibt er in dem Fragment On Life:

The most refined abstractions of logic conduct to a view of life, which, though startling to the apprehension, is, in fact, that which the habitual sense of its repeated combinations has extinguished in us. It strips as it were, the painted curtain from this scene of things. I confess that I am one of those who am unable to refuse my assent to the conclusions of those philosophers who assert, that nothing exists but as it is perceived. It is a decision against which all our persuasions struggle, and we must be long convicted before we can be convinced that the solid universe of external things is, „such stuff as dreams are made of."

Da Vorstellungen aus Berkeley's System sich vor unserm Gedicht bei Byron nicht finden und hier ihr erstmaliges Auftreten zeitlich mit dessen Bekanntwerden mit Shelley zusammenfällt, so dürfen wir sie wohl auf Shelley's Einwirkung zurückführen.

Da nun die Abwesenden nicht wahrgenommen werden können existieren sie nicht, sind tot: the absent are the dead. Der Gedanke „die Abwesenden sind die Toten" wird im folgenden variirt. Die Abwesenden sind die Toten: denn wie diese sind sie kalt, können nicht mehr sein, wie wir sie einst gesehen haben; sie sind verändert und freudlos. Aber wirft der Dichter ein, wenn wir sie nicht vergessen, wenn sie in unserm Gedächtnis fortleben, und wir in ihrem, dann leben sie noch für uns. — Doch fährt er weiter indem er wieder auf die erste Erklärung zurückkommt, da sie von uns getrennt sind, sind sie doch tot für uns. Eines Tages aber wird die Trennung endigen: In the dark union of insensate dust.

Daran schließt sich naturgemäß die Frage, werden wir wenn wir nach dem Tode wieder mit ihnen vereinigt sind, noch unser Wahrnehmungsvermögen haben. Byron stellt diese Frage etwas allgemein:

The underearth in habitants etc.

Und hieran knüpft sich dann die Frage: Wie ist das Leben nach dem Tode beschaffen.

Die letzten fünf Zeilen enthalten die Vorstellung einer Unterwelt, in einer Fassung die von der gewöhnlichen abweicht.

Bei Shelley finden sich ähnliche Vorstellungen davon, so daß hier eine Einwirkung von seiner Seite möglich ist. Er sagt z. B. von den Toten in „On the Punishment of Death"

If they have sensations and apprehensions we no longer participate in them.

In Prometheus III, 3, 112 spricht er von den „uncommunicating dead".

Die Vorstellung von einer Unterwelt findet sich Prometheus I, 1, 150 ff.

For know there are two worlds of life and death:
One that which thou beholdest; but the other
Is underneath the grave.

Da wir nicht blos in wachem Zustande sondern auch im Schlaf Wahrnehmungen haben, die Existenz aber auf Wahrnehmungen beruht so folgt, daß wir im Schlaf, in den Träumen ein Leben haben, das eben so wirklich ist wie das in wachem Zustande. So sagt Shelley:

Marianne's Dream (1817)
— sleep has sights as clear and true
As any waking eyes can view.

Fragment „the desarts of sleep":
I went into the desarts of dim sleep —
That world which, like an unknown wilderness —
Bounds this with its recesses wide and deep.

Von der Wirklichkeit des Lebens im Traum spricht Shelley ferner noch in „Speculations on Metaphysics V".

Byron zeigt sich von diesen Vorstellungen beeinflußt, im Anfang von „Dream":

Our life is twofold: Sleep hath its own world
A boundary between the things misnamed

Death and existence: Sleep hath its own world
And a wide realm wild reality.
And dreams — — — —

— — — — —

They do divide our being; they become
A portion of ourselves. — — —

Wie wir gesehen haben hat der Gedanke, daß das
Individuum eine Modifikation der Substanz ist, bei Byron
und Shelley die Möglichkeit eines Weiterlebens des In=
dividuums nach dem Tode begründet; ebenso natürlich er=
giebt sich hieraus die Idee einer Präexistenz. So bei Shelley:
On the Punishment of Death:
The philosopher is unable to determine whether
our existence in a previous state has affected our present
condition. — — —

Cenci:
The offences of some unremembered world

Prince Aathnese (1817)
— — memories of an antenatal life
Made this where now he dwelt a penal hell.

Byron hat dieses Motiv in: The two Foscari II, 1
— — — — so that
Methinks we must have sinned in some old world
Ant this is hell — — — — —

Wir sehen so bei Shelley und Byron die verschiedensten
Vorstellungen über Leben und Dasein. „Daß wir nichts
wissen können" ist auch bei ihnen das Ergebnis des Forschens
nach Wahrheit. In der Äußerung der daraus entspringenden
Ungewißheit stimmen sie zum Teil überein, so daß eine Ein=
wirkung Shelley's auf Byron auch hier möglich ist. Schon
Wordsworth spricht von:
mystic streams of Life and Death
(Descriptive sketches)

und in Excursion von:
the burthen of the mystery

— — — — — —

Of all this unintelligible world.
Ähnlich sagt Shelley in „On Life":

What is life? — — — How vain is it to think that words can penetrate the mystery of our being! — — — — For what are we? Whence do we come? and whither do we go?

ferner Adonais XXI

> Whence are we, and why are we? of what scene
> The actors and spectators. — — --

Sonnet (1820)

> Thou vainly curious mind which wouldest guess
> Whence thou didst come and wither thou mayst go,

Triumph of Life (1822)

> Show whence I came, and where I am and why.

In gleicher Weise sagt Byron:

Don Juan VI, 58

> What are we and whence came we? What
> shall be
> Our ultimate existence? what's our present?
> Are questions answerless and yet incessant.

Two Foscari II,1

> Mar.                         And that's a mystery
> Doge. All things are so to mortals.

Sardanapalus V 1.

> The labyrinth of mystery, call'd life.

Geheimnisvoll wie das Leben ist auch das Lebens-prinzip. So spricht Shelley von:

> the mysterious principle which regulates the universe

(in On a Future State).

Und in (Hymn to intellectual Beauty) sagt er:

> The awful shadow of some unseen Power
> Floats tho' unseen amongst us.

In gleichem Sinne spricht wohl Byron Manfred I, 1 von einer „mysterious agency".

Da die Substanz für alle Wesen die Quelle des Lebens ist, so sind auch dessen Äußerungen bei allen dieselben:

Queen Mab IV 143 ff.

> Every grain
> Is sentient both in unity and part
> And the minutest atom comprehends

A world of loves and hatreds.

**ibd. II 102**
The passions, prejudices, interests
That sway the meanest being.

**ibd II 931 ff.**
I tell thee that these viewless beings,
Whose mansion is the smallest particle
Of the impassive atmosphere,
Think feel and live like man.

Diese Vorstellungen haben bei Byron wohl auf Stellen gewirkt wie:

**Manfred II, 4**
— the passions, attributes
Of earth and heaven, from which no power,
nor being
Nor breath from the worm upwards is exempt.

**Two Foscari II, 1.**
the rest was nakedness
And lusts, and appetites, and vanities,
The universal heritage.

Es finden sich auch sonst noch viele übereinstimmende Ideen in der Dichtung Byrons und Shelley's, besonders in ihrer Freiheitsdichtung. Hier hat Shelley jedoch kaum auf Byron wirken können. Freiheitliche Ideen finden sich in dessen Dichtung schon lang vor 1816, und zudem war damals die ganze Atmosphäre von ihnen geschwängert. Wenn in dieser Hinsicht irgend eine Einwirkung auf Byron stattgefunden hat, so scheint sie mir von Wordsworth und Southey geschehen zu sein.

Neben den Dichtungen kommen zur Erkenntnis der Weltanschauung Byrons auch noch dessen Briefe in Betracht. Donner hat die in dieser Hinsicht wichtigsten Stellen daraus in seiner Abhandlung angeführt und besprochen (S. 106, 107). Ich kann mir also wohl ersparen, eingehender auf die Briefe einzugehen. Inwieweit die darin ausgesprochenen Ideen und Vorstellungen von Shelley beeinflußt worden sind, wird sich nach dem vorausgehenden ohne weiteres ergeben.

Hiermit ist der erste Teil meiner Aufgabe die Einwirkung Shelley's auf Byron's Weltanschauung zu Ende und ich werde jetzt im folgenden versuchen festzustellen, in wie weit Shelley noch anderweitig auf Byron gewirkt hat.

## Kapitel III.
# Sonstige Einwirkungen Shelley's auf Byron.

Die perſönlichen Beziehungen zwiſchen Byron und Shelley waren, wie nicht anders zu erwarten, beſonders rege während ihres gemeinſamen Aufenthaltes am Genfer See. Infolgedeſſen finden ſich mannigfache Übereinſtimmungen zwiſchen C H III Byrons poetiſchem Tagebuch aus jener Zeit und den teilweiſe von Mrs. Shelley, teilweiſe von Shelley geſchriebenen »Letters written during a residence of three months in the environs of Geneva«. Es iſt natürlich manch-mal ſchwer feſtzuſtellen, inwieweit dieſe Übereinſtimmungen auf die Einwirkung Shelley's zurückgehn, da ſie jedoch für die Entſtehungsgeſchichte mancher Teile von C H III nicht unwichtig ſind, ziehe ich ſie in den Rahmen meiner Unter-ſuchung.

In C H III 73 ſpricht Byron davon, daß er fühlt, wie ſeinem Genius im Verkehr mit der Natur neue Schwingen wachſen:

I look upon the peopled desert past
As on a place of agony and strife
Where for some sin to sorrow I was cast
To act and suffer, but remount at last
With a fresh pinion; which I feel to spring
Though young yet waxing vigorous . . .

Ähnlich ſagt Mrs Shelley im erſten Brief:

I feel as happy as a new fledged bird and hardly care what twig I fly to, so that I may try my new-found wings. Etwas früher ſagt ſie in demſelben Brief:

— — — — as we approach the shore we are saluted by the delightful scent of flowers and new mown grass and the chirp of the grasshopper and the song of the evening birds.

Dieſelbe Scene ſchildert Byron C H III 86 in folgenden Worten:

There breathes a living fragrance from the shore
Of flowers yet fresh with childhood on the ear,

Drops the light trip of the suspended oar
Or chirps the grasshopper one good night
carol more.

Im zweiten Brief schildert uns dann Mrs. Shelley
eines der Gewitter, die während jener Zeit ziemlich zahl-
reich waren:

The thunderstorms that visit us are grander and
more terrific than I have ever seen before. We watch
them as they approach from the opposite side of the
lake; observing the lightning play among the clouds in
various parts of the heavens and dart in jagged figures
upon the piny hight of Jura, dark with the shadow of
the overhanging cloud, while perhaps the sun is shining
cheerily upon us. One night we enjoyed a finer storm
than I had ever before beheld. The lake was lit up, —
the pines on Jura made visible, and all the scene
illuminated for an instant, when a pitchy blackness
succeeded, and the thunder came in frightful bursts over
our heads amid the darkness.

Dasselbe Gewitter schildert Byron C H III 93—96.
An Mrs. Shelley's Darstellung erinnern besonders die
Derse:

How the lit lake shines, a phosphoric sea,
And the big rain comes dancing to the earth!
And now again 'tis black — and now, the glee
Of the loud hills shakes with its mountain mirth,
As if they did rejoice o'er a young earthquake's
birth.

In Shelley's Erstlingswerken bildet die Schilderung
eines Gewitters ein beliebtes Motiv. Gewitterschilderungen
finden sich z. B. in Zastrozzi S. 10, 34, 98, 102. St. Irvyne,
Kapitel I.

Besonders die Schilderung in St. Irvyne zeigt mannigfache Übereinstimmungen mit der in C H III. Natürlich
kann diese Übereinstimmung ganz zufällig sein. Ein Gewitter spielt sich ja immer mehr oder minder auf dieselbe
Weise ab. Da jedoch St. Irvyne in einem eigentümlichen

Verhältnis zu Manfred steht und deshalb selbst das geringste Unzeichen dafür, daß Byron diesen Roman Shelley's gekannt hat, von Bedeutung ist, führe ich die betreffende Stelle hier an:

— — — — — over the blackened expanse of heaven, at intervals was spread the blue lightnings flash; it played upon the granite heights, and with momentary brilliancy disclosed the terrific scenery of the Alps whose gigantic and misshapen summits reddened by the transitory moonbeam were crossed by black fleeting fragments of the tempest clouds. The rain in big drops began to descend, and the thunder peals with louder and more deafening crash, to shake the Zenith, till the long protracted · war, echoing from cavern to cavern died in undistinct murmurs amidst the far extended chain of mountains.

Auf ihren gemeinsamen Ausflügen suchten Byron und Shelley vor allem die Stellen auf die durch Rousseau verewigt worden sind. Ihre Rousseau-Schwärmerei kommt oft in denselben Worten zum Ausdruck. Der blendende Genius Rousseau's erscheint beiden als etwas Zauberhaftes. So sagt Shelley in Brief III:

But Meillerie is indeed enchanted ground were Rousseau no magician.

und Byron spricht von Rousseau C H III 77 als:

-- he who threw enchantment over passion.

Die Gebilde der Phantasie Rousseaus erscheinen ihnen überirdisch. So sagt Shelley an einer andern Stelle in Brief III:

They were created indeed by one mind, but a mind so powerfully bright as to cast a shade of falsehood on the records that are called reality.

Ähnlich Byron C H III:

yet he knew
How to make madness beautiful, and cast
O'er erring deeds and thoughts a heavenly hue
Of words, like sunbeams dazzling as they past
The eyes — — —

Einige Verse weiter unten sagt Byron von Rousseau
(C H III 78).

> But his was not the love of living dame
> Nor of the dead who rise upon our dreams
> But of ideal beauty, which became
> In him existence and o'erflowing teems
> Along his burning page. — — —

### LXXIX

This breathed itself to life in Julie.

Shelley giebt in ähnlicher Weise seiner Bewunderung
Ausdruck:

> I read Julia all day; an overflowing as it now seems.

(Brief III)

Da er an anderer Stelle in ähnlicher Weise seine Bewunderung ausspricht — er sagt in „A Defence of poetry":

> That wonderful o'erflowing of fancy the Pharsalia of
> Lucan —

so rührt wohl das „o'erflowing teems" in Stanze 78
von ihm her. Eine Parallelstelle zu dem Anfang von
Stanze 79 findet sich ebenfalls in Brief III:

> All this might scarcely be; but the imagination
> surely could not forbear to breathe into the most
> inanimate forms some likeness of its own visions.

Eine Stelle in den Briefen aus der sich eine direkte
Beeinflussung Byron's durch Shelley nachweisen läßt, findet
sich in Brief IV. Shelley beschreibt hier einen Ausflug der
von seiner Frau, Miß Clairmont und ihm nach dem Cha-
mounix-Thal unternommen worden war. Kölbing hat
E. St. XXII S. 140 ff. ausführlich hiervon gehandelt. Ich will
das wichtigste von seinen Ausführungen hier wiedergeben.

Shelley schreibt in dem betreffenden Brief u. a.:

> I will not pursue Buffon's sublime but gloomy
> theory — that this globe which we inhabit, will at some
> future period be changed into a mass of frost by the
> encroachment of the polar ice, and of that produced on
> the most elevated points of the earth. Do you who

assert the supremacy of Ahriman imagine him throned among those desolating snows among these palaces of death and frost, so sculptured in this their terrible magnificence by the adamantine hand of necessity, and that he casts around him as the first essays of his final usurpation avalanches torrents, rocks, and thunders, and above all these deadly glaciers, at once the proof and symbols of his reign; — add to this, the degradation of the human species — who in these regions are half deformed or idiotic, and most of whom are deprived of any thing, that can excite interest or admiration.

Man vergleiche hierzu Manfred I. 1:

Voice of the second Spirit.

Montblanc is the monarch of mountains
They crown'd him long ago
On a throne of rocks in a robe of clouds
With a diadem of snow.
Around his waist are forests braced,
The avalanche in his hand;
But ere it fall, that thundering ball
Must pause for my command.
The Glacier's cold and restless mass
Moves onward day by day.
But J am he who bids it pass,
Or with its ice delay.

Kölbing bemerkt hierzu:

„Aus diesen hier citierten Stellen geht zunächst hervor, daß der Inhalt von 9 ff in der Rede des zweiten Geistes auf einer wissenschaftlichen Beobachtung basiert ist; weiter aber, daß sich hier schon die originelle, freilich etwas phan- thastische Idee findet Ahriman throne in der schwindelnden Berghöhe in einem Eispalaste — welche später die Koulissen zu Manfred II, sc. 4 bestimmt hat, ihm werden schon von Shelley die Machtäußerungen zugeschrieben, welche der zweite Geist in Manfred I, sc. 1 sich vindiziert: die Herr- schaft über Lawinen und Gletscher. Und wenn Shelley hier den Kontrast zwischen der häufigen Krüppelhaftigkeit der Bergbewohner einerseits und der grandiosen Alpenwelt andrer-

seits betont, so läßt Byron seinen Helden diese Diskrepanz
gleichfalls hervorheben, nur daß er die ganze elende Menschheit dabei in Betracht zieht, nicht blos die allerdings von
der Natur oft besonders stiefmütterlich behandelten Spröß-
linge der Gebirgsthäler; vgl. Manfreds Monolog Akt 1, sc. 2:

> How beautiful is all this visible world
> How glorious in its action and itself?
> But we, who name ourselves its sovereigns, we,
>
> ... — — — — — — — — — — make
> A conflict of its elements, and breathe
> The breath of degradation and of pride — —

Wie wir bereits gesehen haben liebt es Shelley den
Menschen als Zerstörer der Harmonie der Natur darzustellen.
Ähnlich wie in der oben angeführten Stelle aus den „letters
during a six month's residence in the environs of Geneva"
sagt er in Brief 65:

> But external nature in these delightful regions con-
> trasts with and compensates for the deformity and degra-
> dation of humanity.

Es ist also sehr wohl möglich, daß Byron dieses
Motto von ihm hat.

Kölbing weist ferner noch darauf hin, daß Vers 5 in
der Rede des zweiten Geistes:

> Around his waist are forests braced     [blanc:

sich inhaltlich deckt mit Vers 19 von Shelley's Mont-

> thou doest lie,
> Thy giant brood of pines around the clinging.

und daß Vers 8

> that thundering ball
> Must pause for my command.

an die im Monblanc aufgeworfene Frage erinnert:

> Is this the scene
> Where the old Earthquake - daemon taught her
> Ruin?                    [young

Doch glaube ich, daß Kölbing im letzten Fall etwas
zu weit geht und Übereinstimmungen sieht, wo keine vorhanden sind.

Auf Shelley's Monblanc und die Rede des zweiten
Geistes in Manfred I, 2 hat wohl Coleridges „Hymn before
sunrise in the Vale of Chamouny" vorbildlich gewirkt:

Hast thou a charm to stay the morning star
In his steep course? so long he seems to pause
On thy bald, awful head, O sovran Blanc;
The Arve and Arveiron at thy base
Rave ceaselessly; but thou, most awful form!
Risest from out thy silent, sea of pines
How silently! Around thee and above
Deep is the air and dark, substantial, black,
An ebon mass, methinks thou piercest it
As with a wedge! But when I look again,
It is thine own calm home, thy crystal shrine
Thy habitation from eternity. I gazed upon thee,
Till thou, still present to the bodily sense,
Didst vanish from my thought; entranced in prayer
I worshipped the Invisible alone.

Es finden sich noch anderweitige Übereinstimmungen
zwischen den Briefen Written a residence of six
month's in the environs of Geneva und der Rede des
zweiten Geistes.

Eine Stelle aus Brief I:

— — — — and towering far above, in the midst
of its snowy Alps the majestic Mont Blanc, highest and
queen of all.

und eine aus Brief IV:

— — Mont Blanc was before us — the Alps with
their innumerable glaciers on high all around — — —
forests inexpressibly beautiful — — — overshadowed
our road — — — — Mont Blanc was before us, but
it was covered with cloud; its base furrowed with
dreadful gaps, was seen above

decken sich mit

Montblanc is the monarch of mountains
They crown'd him long ago
On a throne of rocks, in a robe of clouds,

With a diadem of snow.

unb — — quiver to his caverned base —

Man vergleiche ferner noch:

The Glacier's cold and restless mass
Moves onward day by day mit folgenden Stellen
aus Brief IV:

These glaciers flow perpetually into the valley

ibd.     — — — — In these regions every thing
changes and is in motion. This vast mass of
ice has one general progress.

ibd.     The glaciers perpetnally move onward at the
rate of a foot each day

ibd.     Within this last year, these glaciers have
advanced three hundred feet into thevalley.

Shelley spricht also in Brief IV wiederholt von dem naturwissenschaftlichen Phänomen des Dorrückens der Gletscher.

Zwei andere Naturerscheinungen, die Shelley beobachtet
hat und von denen er in Brief IV spricht, sind der Sturz
einer Lawine und ein Bergrutsch:

It was an avalanche. We saw the smoke of its
path among the rocks, and continued to hear at intervals
the bursting of its fall. It fell on the bed of a torrent,
which it displaced, and presently we saw its tawny-
coloured waters also spread themselves over the ravine,
which was their couch.

ibd.

Mont Blanc forms one of the sides of this vale
also, and the other is inclosed by an irregular amphitheatre
of enormous mountains, one of which is in ruins, and
fell fifty years ago into the higher part of the valley:
the smoke of its fall was seen in Piedmont, and people
went from Turin to investigate whether a volcano had
not burst among the Alps. It continued falling many
days, spreading, with the shock and thunder of its ruin,
consternation into the neighbouring vales.

Von einem ähnlichen Naturereignis ist die Rede in
Manfred I, 2:

Mountains have fallen,
Leaving a gap in the clouds, and with the shock
Rocking their Alpine brethren; filling up
The ripe green valleys with destruction's splinters;
Damming the rivers with a sudden dash,
Which crush'd the waters into mist, and made
Their fountains find another channel —

Shelley war, wie aus den angeführten Stellen hervor·
geht, ein ziemlich scharfer Beobachter der Natur. Er hat
sich eingehend mit verschiedenen naturwissenschaftlichen Pro·
blemen beschäftigt, u. a. fühlte er sich sehr durch die Astro·
nomie angezogen. Infolge dessen spielen die Sterne eine
große Rolle in seiner Dichtung. Byron wurde von Shelley
in den großartigen Schilderungen der Sternenwelt und des
Alls in Kain beeinflußt. Es möge zunächst eine Anzahl
von Stellen aus Shelley folgen, in denen von den Sternen
die Rede ist

Noten zu Queen Mab I:

The plurality of words, — the indefinite immensity
of the universe is a most awful subject of contemplation.

— — — — — — —

That which appears only like a thin and silvery
cloud streaking the heaven, is in effect composed of
innumerable clusters of suns, each shining with its own
light, and illuminating numbers of planets that revolve
around them.

Millions and millions of suns ars ranged around
us, all attended by innumerable worlds, yet calm regular
and harmonious, all keeping the paths of immutable
necessity.

On the Devil, and Devils.

— —· — — prodigious orb of elemental light,
which sustains, and animates that multitude of inhabited
globes, in whose company this earth revolves.

Stellen aus Shelley's Dichtung in denen er von den
Sternen spricht sind:

Queen Mab I 331 ff.

Seemed it, that the chariot's way

Lay through the midst of an immense concave,
Radiant with million constellations, tinged
With shades of infinite colour,
And semicircled with a belt
Flashing incessant meteors.

Queen Mab I 250 ff.

Earth's distant orb appeared
The smallest light that twinkles in the heaven
Whilst round the chariot's way
Innumerable systems rolled,
And countless spheres diffused
An ever-varying glory.
It was a sight of wonder: some
Were horned liked the crescent moon;
Some shed a mild and silver beam
Like Hesperus over the western sea;
Some dash'd athwart with trains of flame
Like worlds to death and ruin driven;
Some shone like suns — — —

Laon and Cythna I 49

                  with many a golden beam
The thronging constellations rush in clouds
Paving with fire the sky and the marmoreal
                          floods.
Prometheus I, 1, 163 ff.
Then see those million worlds which burn
Around us.                 [and roll

With a Guitar to Jane (1817)

That seldom-heard mysterious sound
Which, driven on its diurnal round
As it floats through boundless day,
Our world enkindles on its way.

Prologue to Hellas (𝔣𝔯𝔞𝔤𝔪𝔢𝔫𝔱) 1821

In the blue glow of hyaline
Golden worlds revolve and shine.
In — — -- — ··· — flight
From every point of the Infinite

Like a thousand dawns on a single night
The splendours rise and spread.
And through thunder and darkness dread,
Light and music are radiated,
And, in their pavilioned chariots led
By living wings, high overhead.

ibd. The fairest of those wandering isles that gem
The sapphire space of interstellar air
That green and azure sphere, that earth en-
wrapped
Less in the beauty of its tender light
Than in an atmosphere of living spirit.
The giant Powers move,
Gloomy or bright as the thrones they fill.

ibd. The innumerable worlds of golden light
Which are my empire, and the least of them
— — — which thou wouldst redeem from me?
Know'st thou not then my portion?
Or wouldst rekindle the — — — strife
Which our great Father then did arbitrate
When he assigned to his competing sons
Each his apportioned realm?

Diese Stelle ist besonders wichtig; denn sie zeigt uns
die Einwirkung Shelley's auf die Gestaltung von „Kain"
nach ihren zwei Hauptrichtungen hin — Handlung:
Kampf der beiden Prinzipe — Scenerie: Sternenwelt und
All. Man könnte beinahe versucht sein daraus zu schließen,
daß sich Shelley mit dem Gedanken einer Dichtung wie
Kain trug, die Keime dazu sind jedenfalls bei ihm vorhanden
gewesen wie aus der obigen Stelle und dem andern was
bereits mit Bezug auf „Kain" gesagt worden ist, hervorgeht. Hierauf scheint auch noch Fragment 36 in Rossetti's
Ausgabe hinzuweisen, wo von dem Losbrechen Luzifers von
seinen Ketten gesprochen wird.

Man vergl. ferner noch:
Prometheus IV, 236. 270. 469.
Laon and Cythna VI 32. Witch of Atlas 46, 47.

Befonbers wichtig für Shelley's Sternenbichtung ift
Ode to Heaven:

First Spirit:
Palace roof of cloudness nights!
Paradise of golden lights!
Deep, immeasurable, vast,
Which art now, and which wert then!
Of the present and the past,
Of the eternal where and when,
Presence-chamber, temple. home
Ever-canopying dome
Of acts and ages yet to come!
Glorious shapes have life in thee,
Earth, and all earth's company;
Living globes which ever throng
Thy deep chasms and wildernesses;
And green worlds that glide along;
And zwift stars with flashing tresses.
And icy moons most cold and bright
And mighty suns beyond the night,
Atoms of intensest light.

Third Spirit
Peace! the abyss is wreathed with scorn
At your presumption, atom — born!
What is heaven? and what are ye
Who its brief expanse inherit?
What are suns and spheres which flee
With the instinct of that spirit
Of which ye are but a part?
Drops which Nature's mighty heart
Drives through thinnest veins. Depart!
What is heaven? a globe of dew,
Filling in the morning new
Some eyed flower whose young leaves waken
On an unimagined world!
Constellated suns unshaken,
Orbits measureless, are furled
In that frail and fading sphere
With ten millions gathered there,
To tremble gleam and disappear.

Der Einfluß Shelley's auf Byron in der Darftellung
bes Alls und ber Sternenwelt zeigt fich befonbers in folgenben
Stellen.

Kain I, 1        but thou seem'st
Like an ethereal night, where long white clouds
Streak the deep purple, and unnumber'd stars
Spangle the wonderful mysterious vault
With things that look as if they would be suns.
(vgl. Q. M. I 225 ff)

Kain II, 1
    Yon small blue circle, swinging in far ether
    With an inferior circlet near it . . .
ibd.   And if there should be
    Worlds greater than thine own, inhabited
    — — — — — — — —
    All living, and all doom'd to death, — —
           (vgl. Ode to Heaven, Third Spirit)

ibd.              Oh, thou beautiful
And unimaginable ether! and
Ye multiplying masses of increased
And still increasing lights! what are ye? what
Is this blue wilderness of interminable
Air, where ye roll along — — —
— — — —
Is your course measured for ye? Or do ye
Sweep on in your unbounded revelry
Through an aërial universe of endless
Expansion — — -- --

ibd.
And some emitting sparks, and some displaying
Enormous liquid plains, and some begirt
With luminous belts, and floating moons.

Kain II. 2
— — — the huge brilliant orbs which swung
So thickly in the upper air — — — —
- — — — — — —
-  - — swelling into palpable immensity
Of matter, which seem'd made for life to dwell on
Rather than life itself.


Byron weiſt hier die von Shelley in Ode to Heaven
ausgeſprochene Anſicht von der Allbelebtheit der Himmels-
körper halb zurück.

ibd.  Myriads of starry worlds of which our own
      Is the dim and remote companion, in
      Infinity of life. — — —

Kain III, 1.                              The dead,
      The immortal, the unbounded, the omnipotent,
      The overpowering mysteries of space —
      The innumerable worlds that were and are —
      A whirlwind of such overwhelming things,
      Suns, moons, and earths upon their loudvoiced
      Singing in thunder round me. — —    [spheres

Auch in Manfred finden sich Spuren der Einwirkung
Shelley's in dieser Hinsicht:
      Manfred I, 1

          The burning wreck of a demolish'd world
          A wandering hell in the eternal space;

ibd. Rede des siebten Geistes:

          The star which rules thy destiny
          Was ruled ere earth began by me.
          It was a world as fresh and fair
          As e'er resolved round sun in air;
          Its course was free and regular,
          Space bosom'd not a lovelier star;
          The hour arrived — and it became
          A wandering mass of shapeless flame,
          A pathless comet, and a curse
          The menace of the universe;
          Still rolling on with innate force,
          Without a sphere, without a course,
          A bright deformity on high,
          The monster of the upper sky.

Der Einfluß Shelley's auf die Scenerie in „Kain",
wenn ich es so nennen darf, scheint mir noch weiter zu
gehn. So finden sich für den Flug Luzifers und Kains
durch die Luft verschiedene Vorbilder in Shelley's Dichtung z. B.

      Epithalamion of Ravaillac and Charlotte Corday
III (1810)

Methought, enthroned upon a silvery cloud,
Which floated mid a strange and brilliant light,
My form, upborne by viewless ether, rode,
And spurned the lessening realms of earthly night.
What heavenly notes burst on my ravished ears!
What beauteous spirits met my dazzled eye!
Hark louder swells the music of the spheres —
More clear the forms of speechless blith float
                                              by —
And heavenly gestures suit etherial melody.


Ferner der Flug, den Queen Mab mit dem Geift der
Janthe unternimmt (Queen Mab I):

The magic car moved on
The night was fair, and countless stars
Studded heaven's dark-blue vault.
— .. —  - .. —

The chariot seemed to fly
Through the abyss of an immense concave,
Radiant with million constellations, tinged
With shades of infinite colour,
And semicircled with a belt
Flashing incessant meteors.
— —  — - - —

The magic car moved on.
Earth' s distant orb appeared
The smallest light that twincles in the heavens;
Whilst round the chariot's way
Innumerable systems rolled,
And countless spheres diffused
An ever-varying glory.    .
It was a sight of wonder: some
Were hornèd like the crescent moon;
Some shed a mild and silver beam,
Like Hesperus o'er the western sea,
Some dashed athwart with trains of flame,
Some shone like stars, and, as the chariot passed,
Bedimmed all other light.


Von einer Fahrt in die Sternenwelt ift ebenfalls die
Rede Laon and Cythna I, 52:

We came to a vast hall whose glorious roof
Was diamond, which had drunk the light-
⠀⠀⠀⠀⠀⠀⠀⠀⠀⠀ning's sheen
In darkness, and now pour'd it through the woof
Of spell-in woven clouds hung there to screen
Its blinding splendour. Through such veil was
⠀⠀⠀⠀⠀⠀⠀⠀⠀⠀seen
That work of subtlest power, divine and rare;
Orb above orb, with starry shapes between,
And horned moons and meteors strange and fair;
On night-black columns poised — one hollow
⠀⠀⠀⠀⠀⠀⠀⠀⠀⠀hemisphere.

Das Motiv eines fluas durch die £üfte findet fich
außerdem noch in Triumph of Life. Auch in dem Gedicht
To Constantia, singing (1817) findet fich eine Stelle, der
diefes Motiv zu Grunde liegt.

The cope of heaven seems rent and cloven
By the enchantment of thy strain,
And on my shoulders wings are woven,
To follow its sublime career
Beyond the mighty moons that wane
Upon the verge of Nature's utmost sphere,
Till the world's shadowy walls are passed and
⠀⠀⠀⠀⠀⠀⠀⠀⠀⠀disappear.

Durch einen Dergleich der hier aus Shelley angeführten
Stellen mit Kain Akt II ergiebt fich fofort, daß fie Dorbild
dazu waren.

Auch das Motiv von der Phantomenwelt hat Byron
wohl von Shelley. Bei diefem erfcheint eine ähnliche
Schattenwelt in:

Daemon of the world I 253 ff:
⠀⠀A while the Spirit paused in ecstasy
⠀⠀Yet soon she saw, as the vast spheres swept by,
⠀⠀Strange things within their belted orbs appear
⠀⠀Like animated frenzies, dimly moved
⠀⠀Shadows and skeletons, and fiendly shapes . . .

Man vergleiche hierzu:
Cain II, I

Cain.      How the ligths recede
  Where fly we?
Lucifer.    To the world of phantoms, which
Are beings past, and shadows still to come.

Jn Byron's Kain wird ferner der Hades als Schatten-
bild der Welt der Lebenden gedacht. Die Schatten werden
weiterlebend gedacht:

Kain II, 2
Cain         — — — — what are ye
  Live ye, ore have ye lived
Lucifer        Somewhat of both.

Byron kann zu dieser Vorstellung von der antiken
vom Hades aus gekommen sein. Shelley hat im Prometheus
eine ähnliche Vorstellung von der Unterwelt, so daß sein
Einfluß in dieser Hinsicht immerhin nicht unmöglich ist:

Prometheus I, 1, 195
For know there are two worlds of life and death
One that which thou beholdest; but the other
Is underneath the grave, where do inhabit
The shadows of all forms that think and live
Till death unite them and they part no more.

Weitere Stellen im Kain bei denen noch der Einfluß
Shelley's möglich war sind:

Kain II, 2.
What are these mighty phantoms which I see
Floating around me?
ibd.  Behold these phantoms! they were once Material
as thou art.

Man vergleiche hierzu Triumph of Life (1822):
The mighty phantoms of an elder day.

Eine weitere Übereinstimmung findet sich noch zwischen
Kain III 1:

```
Adah                           'Tis scarcely
     Two hours since ye departed: two long hours
     To me but only hours upon the sun.
Cain.  And yet I have approached that sun, and
                                    seen
     Worlds which he once shone on, and never more
     Shall light; and worlds he never lit: methought
     Years had roll'd o'er my absence.
```

und Laon and Cythna III, 2:

```
     Two hours, whose migthy circle did embrace
     More time than might make grey the
                                    infant world,
     Rolled thus, a weary and tumultuous space.
```

Von andern Einwirkungen Shelley's auf Byron find noch zu erwähnen der auf Byron's Gedicht Darkness. Ackermann weift darauf hin (Anglia, Beiblatt VIII S. 15) daß Laon and Cythna auf Darkness eingewirkt haben kann. Wenngleich Laon and Cythna erft 1817, Darkness dagegen bereits 1816 entftanden ift, kann Shelley doch hier auf Byron gewirkt haben, denn Scenen der Zerftörung wie fie hier gefchildert werden, find bei ihm ein ftehendes Motiv. Außer den Stellen in Laon and Cythna (III 22 A shoreless sea, a sky sunless and planetless und VI 42 ff) werden Scenen der Zerftörung noch gefchildert in Ode to Liberty (1820), Vision of the sea (1820), Summer and Winter (1820). Man vergleiche hierzu auch das was Kölbing in feiner Byron-Ausgabe über Darkness fagt. Hat Shelley in diefer Hinficht wirklich auf Byron gewirkt, fo wäre noch auf den Spruch von First Destiny in Manfred II, 3 hinzuweifen:

```
     The city lies sleeping
     The morn to deplore it
     May dawn ont it weeping:
     The black plague flew o'er it —
     Thousands lie lowly;
     Tens of thousands shall perish —
     The living shall fly from
     The sick they should cherish;
     But nothing can vanquish
```

The touch that they die from.
Sorrow and anguish,
And evil and dread
Envelope a nation,
The blest are the dead,
Who see not the sight
Of their own desolation.

Eine Parallele hierzu findet sich:

Prometheus I Chorus of Furies

O ye who shake hills with the scream of your
                                    mirth
When cities sink howling in ruin: and ye
Who with wingless footsteps trample the sea
And close upon Shipwreck and Famine's track
Sit chattering with joy on the foodless wreck,
Come, come, come!
Leave the bed, low, cold, and red,
Strewed beneath a nation dead.
Leave the hatred, as in ashes
Fire is left for future burning.

Allerdings ist es auch umgekehrt möglich, daß Shelley
hier von Byron beeinflußt wurde.

Daß Byron und Shelley an den politischen Geschicken
Italiens warmen Anteil nahmen ist bekannt. Auch in
ihrer Dichtung sprechen sie diese Teilnahme für das unglückliche
Land, dessen Gastfreundschaft sie genossen wiederholt aus. So
Shelley in:

Ode to Naples Epode I β (1820)

Hear ye the march as of the Earth-born Forms
Arrayed against the ever-living Gods?
The crash and darkness of a thousand storms
Bursting their inaccessible abodes
        Of crags and thunder clouds?
See ye the banners blazoned to the day,
Inwrought with emblems of barbaric pride?
Dissonant threats kill silence far away;
The serene heaven which wraps our Eden wide
        With iron light is dyed.

The anarchs of the North lead forth their legions,
Like chaos o'er creation, uncreating;
And hundred tribes nourished on strange religions
And lawles slaveriess.   Down the aërial regions
    Of the white Alps, desolating,
Famished wolves that bide no waiting
Blotting the glowing footsteps of old glory,
Trampling our columned cities into dust,
On Beauty's corse to sickness satiating —
    They come! The fields they tread look black
                      and hoary
With fire — from their red feet the streams
                    run gory!

Shelley's Vorbild war hier zum Teil wohl das berühmte Sonnet Filicaja's:

Italia, Italia
O tu cui feo la sorte etc.

Byron hat diefes Sonnet in C H IV. 42, 43 überfetzt. Jn Deformed Transformed II. 1 Chorus of spirits in the air finden fich Stellen in denen ähnliche Gedanken aus· gefprochen werden, die jedoch der Faffung Shelley's in Epode I 3. näher ftehn:

I

'Tis the morn, but dim and dark
Whither flies the silent lark?
Whither shrinks the clouded sun?
Is the day indeed begun.
Nature's eye is melancholy
O'er the city high and holy:
But without there is a din
Should arouse the saints within,
And revive the heroic ashes.
Round which yellow Tiber dashes.
Oh ye seven hills awaken,
Ere your very base be shaken!

Near — and near — and nearer still,
As the earthquake saps the hill,
First with trembling hollow motion,
Like a scarce awaken'd ocean
Then with stronger shock and louder,
Till the rocks are crush'd to powder.

\* \* \*

V

Onward sweep the varied nations!
Famine long has dealt their rations.
To the wall, with hate and hunger
Numerous as wolves and stronger.

Kölbing weist (E. St. XXII S. 142) darauf hin, daß die in Manfred sich zeigende pantheistische Weltanschauung auf Shelley zurückgeht. Da wie ich gezeigt habe das Auftreten des Pantheismus in Byron's Dichtung überhaupt auf Shelley's Einwirkung zurückgeht, so brauche ich den Pantheismus in Manfred und dessen Verhältnis zu Shelley wohl nicht näher zu untersuchen. Die Einwirkung Shelley's auf Manfred geht jedoch weiter. Auch auf die Person Manfred's erstreckt er sich. Wie Byron schwebte auch Shelley das Ideal eines Übermenschen vor. Zastrozzi Wolfstein, Ginotti, Prometheus, Prince Athanese sind nur Variationen derselben übermenschlichen Idealgestalt, die in Prometheus ihre vollendetste Gestaltung erfahren hat. Anfangs hat der Übermensch Shelley's etwas finsteres, dämonenhaftes an sich. Erst in Prince Athanese ist dieses ganz geschwunden. Es wäre nun sehr interessant die Entwicklung der Ideen vom Übermenschen bei Shelley bis zu Prometheus und bei Byron bis zu Manfred darzustellen und zu untersuchen inwieweit der Übermensch Shelley's auf die Gestaltung des Byron'schen eingewirkt hat, doch kann dies nicht meine Aufgabe sein.

Shelley hat wohl ferner noch auf die Entstehung
Manfred's dadurch eingewirkt, daß er Byron mit Goethe's
Fauft bekannt machte, seine Haupteinwirkung auf Manfred
kam jedoch von einer ganz andern Seite her, von seinem
Roman St. Irvyne or the Rosicrucian. Darzulegen wie
dies geschah, soll der letzte Teil meiner Aufgabe sein.

## Kapitel IV.
# Shelley's Roman St. Irvyne als Quelle zu Manfred.

St. Irvyne or the Rosicrucian ist ein ziemlich abstrufes
Erzeugnis der Phantafie oder beffer gesagt der Feder Shelley's.
Forman glaubt (Prose works of Percy Bysshe Shelley
B.I. editor's preface S XII ff) St. Irvyne gehe auf zwei
von Shelley ziemlich unbehülflich zusammengefügte deutsche
Erzählungen zurück, deren Faffung zur Zeit jedoch nicht
bekannt ist. Dowden nimmt (Life of Shelley S. 94) diese
Ansicht Forman's nicht so ohne weiteres an. Nachdem er
deffen Hypotefe befprochen fährt er fort:

In a letter from Shelley to Hogg — — — occurs
the enigmatic sentence, Why will you compliment St.
Irvyne? I never saw Delisle's, but mine must have been
pla — Shall we complete the word? — „plagiarized."
And does Shelley mean that his German original must
have been plagiarized from some romance or drama by
Delisle?

Was die Quelle zu St. Irvyne war wird dadurch
nicht klarer. So viel scheint mir jedoch festzustehn daß
St. Irvyne eine Kombination zweier Erzählungen ist.

Zwischen St. Irvyne und Manfred finden sich nun so
viele und so auffällige Übereinstimmungen, daß sie mir diesen
Roman als die oft vermutete und oft gesuchte Quelle
„Manfred's" erscheinen laffen. Eine nähere Unterfuchung

über die Manfred-Frage bis Dato anzustellen kann nicht meine Aufgabe sein. Ich werde deshalb sofort in medias res gehen und die übereinstimmenden Stellen zwischen Manfred und St. Irvyne anführen.

Eine solche Stelle findet sich gleich am Anfang von St. Irvyne Kap. I. Es wird hier zunächst das Toben eines Gewitters in den Alpen geschildert; dann heißt es weiter:

„In this scene, then, at this horrible and tempesteous hour, without one existent earthly being whom he might claim as friend, without one resource to which he might fly as an asylum from the horrors of neglect and poverty stood Wolfstein: — he gazed upon the conflicting elements, his youthful figure réclined against a jutting granite rock; he cursed his wayward destiny and implored the Almighty of Heaven to permit the thunderbolt, with crash terrific and exterminating, to descend upon his head, that a being useless to himself and to society might no longer by his existence, mock Him who ne'er made ought in vain. „And what so horrible crimes have I committed", exclaimed Wolfstein, driven to impiety by desperation, „what crimes which merit punishment like this?" . . . . As thus he spoke, a more terrific paroxysm of excessive despair revelled through every vain; his brain swam around in wild confusion and, rendered delirious by excess of misery, he started from his flinty seat and swiftly hastened towards the precipice, which yawned widely beneath his feet. „For what then should I longer drag on the galling chain of existence?" cried Wolfstein; and his impious expression was borne onwards by the hot and sulphurous thunderblast.

Diese schreckliche Scene wird im folgenden noch variiert und weiter ausgemalt. Wolfstein sinkt zuletzt besinnungslos zu Boden. Dieselbe Scene erscheint noch zweimal im weitern Verlauf des Romans. In Kapitel X erzählt Ginotti dem Wolfstein sein vergangenes Leben, sein Forschen nach dem Geheimnis des Lebens und die Vergiftung seines Beleidigers. Er fährt dann fort:

„Here in the bitterness of my heart, I cursed that nature and chance which I believed in; and in a paroxysmal frenzy of contending passions cast myself, in desperation, at the foot of a lofty ash-tree, which reared its fantastic form over a torrent which dashed below.

It was midnight; far had I wandered from Salamanca; the passions which agitated my brain, almost to delirium had added strength to my nerves, and swiftness to my feet; but after many hours' incessant walking, I began to feel fatigued. -- — — — — — The sky was véiled by a thick covering of clouds. — — — — — — — — — — — — — I gazed on the torrent, foaming beneath my feet — — — — — 'T was then that I contemplated self-destruction. I had almost plunged into the tide of death — — — when the soft sound of a bell from a neigh bouring convent, was wafted in the stillness of the night.

Der Sturm der Verzweiflung Ginottis legt sich unter dem befänftigenden Einfluß der Glockentöne. Er sinkt erschöpft zu Boden und schläft ein. Im Schlaf hat er folgenden Traum.

I dreamed that I stood on the brink of a most terrific precipice, far, far above the clouds, amid whose dark forms, which lowered beneath, was seen the dashing of a stupendous cataract; its roarings were born to mine ear by the blast of night — · — — — I saw the dark clouds pass by, borne by the impetuosity of the blast, yet felt no wind myself. Methought darkly gleaming forms rode on their almost palpable prominences.

Diese drei angeführten Stellen sind offenbar nur Variationen ein und derselben Original-Situation die sich aus ihnen ohne Schwierigkeit zurückkonstruieren läßt. Man vergleiche nun dazu Manfred Akt I Szene II. Die Bühnenan- weifung Manfred alone upon the cliffs stimmt mit der Erzählung in St. Irvyne: „in this scene" u. f. w. ziemlich übrein. Ebenso ein Teil des folgenden Monologs:

And you, ye crags, upon whose extreme edge
I stand, and on the torrent's brink beneath
Behold the tall pines dwindled as to shrubs
In dizziness of distance; when a leap,
A stir, a motion, even a breath, would bring
My breast upon its rocky bosom's bed

To rest for ever — wherefore do I pause?
I feel the impulse -- yet I do not plunge;
I see the peril — yet do not recede;
And my brain reels — and yet my foot is firm;
There is a power upon me which withholds,
And makes it my fatality to live;

In der Verfion I von St. Irvyne legt fid) dann der
Aufruhr der Elemente nachdem Wolfftein befinnungslos zu
Boden gefunken ift. Es heißt dann weiter Distant sounds
of song are borne on the breeze: the sounds approach.
Mönche, die einen Toten zu Grabe tragen, kommen heran
und finden Wolfftein. In der zweiten Verfion wird wie bereits
erwähnt Ginotti durch den Klang der Klofterglocke von der
Ausführung feines Vorhabens abgehalten. Von dem
Glockenklang heißt es weiter an der betreffenden Stelle:

It struck a chord in unison with my soul: it
vibrated on the secret springs of rapture.

Die Situation im Manfred hat auch hiemit eine
gewiffe wenn auch entfernte Ähnlichkeit.

Hark! the note
The shephard's pipe in the distance heard.
The natural music of the mountain reed
u. f. w.

Auch der Ausbruch der Verzweiflung bei Wolfftein
und Manfred zeigt unverkennbare Ähnlichkeit. Von Wolfftein
wird gefagt:

— — — he cursed his wayward destiny and
implored the Almighty of Heaven to permit the thunderbolt,
with crash terrific and exterminating, to descend upon
his head — — —

Ähnliches wünfcht Manfred in feiner Verzweiflung:
Ye toppling crags of ice!
Ye avalanches, whom a breath draws down
mountainous o'erwhelming, come and
[crush me!

Ebenſo wird ihre Qual in ähnlicher Weiſe geſchildert. Wolffſtein ruft aus:

Ah dissolution! thy pang is blunted by the hard hand of long-protraited suffering — suffering unspeakable, indiscribable.

Manfred ſagt von ſich:
Now furrowed o'er
With wrinkles, plough'd by moments not by years
And hours all tortured into ages.

Die Ähnlichkeit der Situationen in St. Irvyne und Manfred wird noch größer inſofern als auch in Manfred ein Gewitter losbricht.

The mists boil up around the glaciers, clouds
Rise curling fast beneath me, white and sul-
phury
Like foam from the roused ocean of deep Hell.

Man vergleiche zu dem vorausgehenden noch Shelley's Gedicht Despair (1810), in dem ein ähnlicher Ausbruch der Verzweiflung beſchrieben iſt.

I.

And canst thou mock mine agony, thus calm
In cloudless radiance Queen of silver night?
Can you, ye flowerets spread your perfumed balm
Mid pearly gems of dew that shine so bright?
And you wild winds, thus can you sleep so still,
Whilst throbs the tempest of my breast so high?
And in the eternal mansions of the sky
Can the directors of the storm in powerless
silence lie?

II

Hark. I hear the music of the Zephir's wing!
Louder it floats along the unruffled sky!
Some fairy sure has touched the viewless string!
Now faint in distant air the murmurs die —
A while it stills the tide of agony.
Now, now, it loftier swells! again stern woe
Arises with the awakening melody;
Again fierce torments such as demons know,
In bitterer, feller tide on this torn bosom flow.

## III

Arise ye sightless spirits of the storm,
Ye unsèen minstrels of the aërial song!
Pour the fierce tide around this lonely form,
And roll the tempest's wildest swell along!
Dart the red lightning, wing the forked flash
Pour from thy cloud-formed hills the thunder's
                                              roar,
Arouse the whirlwind, and let ocean dash
In fiercest tumult on the rocking shore!
Destroy this life or let earth's fabric be no more.

## IV

Yes every tie that links me here is dead.
Mysterious Fate, thy mandate I obey:
I come terrific Power, J come away.
Then o'er this ruined soul let spirits of hell
In triumph laughing wildly mock its pain
And, though with direst pangs mine heartstrings
                                             swell,
I'll echo back their deadly yells again,
Cursing the Power that ne'er made aught in vain

Überhaupt ift die Stimmung in den Posthumous Fragments of Margaret Nicholson vielfach der in St. Irvyne ähnlich.

Eine weitere Ähnlichfeit ift zwischen der dritten Derflon in St. Irvyne und andern Stellen im Manfred vorhanden. Ihrer Wichtigfeit halber muß ich diese Stelle ihrem ganzen Umfange nach anführen. Es heißt hier im Unschluß an den bereits citierten Teil.

Whilst thus I stood gazing on the expansive gulf which yawned before me, methought a silver sound stole on the quietude of night. The moon became as bright as polished silver, and each star sparkled with scintillations of inexpressible whiteness. Pleasing images stole imperceptibly upon my senses, when a ravishingly sweet strain of dulcet melody seemed to float around — — — — — — Suddenly whilst yet the full strain swelled along the empyrean sky, the mist in one place seemed to depart, and, through it, to roll clouds of deepest crimson. Above them, and seemingly reclining on the viewless air was a form of most exact and superior symmetry. Rays of brilliancy surpassing expression, fell from his burning eye, and the emanations from his countenance tinted the transparent clouds below with silver light. The phantasm advanced towards me, it seemed then to my imagination, that his figure was born on the sweet strain of music which filled the circumambient air. In a voice which was fascination itself the being addressed me saying, Wilt thou come with me? wilt thou be mine?! I felt a decided wish never to be his. — 'No, No I unhesitatingly cried, with a feeling which no language can either explain or describe. No sooner had I uttered these words, than methought a sensation of deadly horror chilled my sickening frame; an earthquake rocked the precipice beneath my feet; the beautiful being vanished: clouds as of chaos rolled around, and from their dark masses flashed incessant meteors. I heard a deafening noise on every side; it appeared like the dissolution of nature, the bloodred moon whirled from her sphere and sank beneath the horizon. My neck was grasped firmly, and turning round in an agony of horror, I beheld a form more hideous than the imagination of man is capable of portraying. whose proportions, gigantic and deformed, were seemingly blackened by the inerasible traces of the thunder bolts of God: yet in its hideous and detestible countenance. though seemingly far different, I thought, I could recognise that of the lovely vision: Wretch! it exclaimed in a voice of exulting thunder; saidst thou, that thou wouldst not be mine? Ah! tho art mine beyond redemption! and I triumph in the conviction that no power can ever make thee otherwise.

Die Lage ist also kurz die: Ginotti sieht sich im Traume am Rande eines Abgrundes. Eine wunderbar schöne Gestalt erscheint und fragt ihn: Wilt thou come with me? wilt thou be mine? Er antwortet mit nein. Die Gestalt verschwindet. Bis hierher stimmt der Traum Ginotti's im allgemeinen mit Scene II im zweiten Akt des „Manfred" überein. Die Scenerie ist hier: A lower valley in the Alps -- A cataract — Enter Manfred. Manfred

beſchwört die Fee der Alpen. Sie erſcheint ihm in ihrer
überirdiſchen Schönheit. Er erzählt ihr ſein Leben und
Leiden.

Dann heißt es weiter:

Witch.                     It may be
          That I can aid thee
Man.                     To do this thy power
          Must wake the dead, or lay me low with them
          Do so — in any shape — in any hour —
          Whith any torture — so it be the last.
Witch. That is not in my province; but if thou
          Wilt swear obedience to my will, and do
          My bidding, it may help thee to thy wishes.
Man. I will not swear — Obey! and whom? the spirit
          Whose presence I command, and be the slave
          Of those, who served me — Never!
Witch.                     Is this all?
          Hast thou no gentler answer? Yet bethink thee,
          And pause ere thou rejectest.
Man.                     I have said it
Witch. Enough — I may retire then — say!
Man.                     Retire!
          (The Witch disappears.)

Es zeigt ſich in dieſer Scene noch eine weitere
Übereinſtimmung mit St. Irvyne. Ginotti erzählt in Kap. X.
des Romans ſein früheres Leben. Er ſagt hier:

From my earlist youth, before it was quenched by
complete satiation, curiosity, and a desire of unveiling
the latent mysteries of nature, was the passion by which
all the other emotions of my mind were intellectually organized.

Dieſe Stelle hat Shelley dann im Alaſtor weiter
ausgeführt. Er apoſtrophiert hier die Natur in folgender
Weiſe:

Mother of this unfathomable world!
Favour my solemn song, for I have loved
Thee ever, and thee only; I have watched
Thy shadow, and the darkness of thy steps,
And my heart ever gazes on the depth

Of thy deep mysteries. I have made my bed
In charnels and on coffins, where black death
Keeps record of the trophies won from thee,
Hoping to still these obstinate questionings
Of thee and thine by forcing some lone ghost
Thy messenger, to render up the tale
Of what we are. In lone and silent hours,
When night makes a weird sound of its own
                                    stillness,
Like an inspired and desperate alchymist
Staking his very life on some dark hope,
Have I mixed awful talk and asking looks
With my most innocent love

Ähnlich in Hymn to intellectual Beauty (1816)

While yet a boy, I sought for ghosts and sped
Through many a listening chamber, cave and ruin
And starlight wood, with fearful steps pursuing
Hopes of high talk with the departed dead.


Man vergleiche nun zu diesen Stellen was Manfred (Af II, Scene 2) von sich sagt:

And then I dived,
In my lone wanderings, to the caves of death,
Searching its cause in its effect; and drew
From wither'd bones and skulls and heaped up dust
Conclusions most forbidden. Then I pass'd
The nights of years in sciences untaught,
Save in the old time; and with time and toil,
And terrible ordeal, and such penance
As in itself hath power upon the air,
And spirits that do compass air and earth,
Space and the peopled infinite. I made
Mine eyes familiar with Eternity,
Such as before me, did the Magi. and,
He who from out their fountain dwellings raised
Eros and Anteros, at Gadera,
As I do thee.


Eine Parallele zu der Stelle in Alastor

Have I mixed awful talk and asking looks
With my most innocent love. — — —

7

findet sich Manfred III 3. Hier sagt Manuel:

Count Manfred was, as now, within his tower, —
How occupied, we know not, but with him
The sole companion of his wanderings
And watchings — her, whom of all earthly
things,
That lived, the only thing he seem'd to love, —

Auch Alastor 75—105 und der Anfang der Erzählung, die Manfred der Alpenfee von seinem frühern Leben giebt, weisen mannigfache Berührungspunkte auf. Zum Teil ähnelt die Situation der im Anfang von C. H. I. Byron braucht also hier nicht von Shelley beeinflußt gewesen sein. Man kann sogar vielleicht im Gegenteil hier eine Beeinflussung Shelley's durch den Anfang von C. H. I. annehmen.

Die Erzählung Ginotti's von seinem Traum ist sicher das Vorbild einer andern Stelle in Alastor gewesen. Es wird hier erzählt (Vers 149 ff) wie der Held des Gedichtes nach langer Wanderung ermattet einschläft. Er träumt von einer schönen Frauengestalt die ein wunderbares Lied singt. Er will sie umfassen. Da erwacht er. Die Wundererscheinung ist verschwunden und Verzweiflung ergreift ihn. Dieselbe Scene spielt sich in Manfred erster Akt, Scene I ab. Der 7te-Geist, der Genius Manfreds wie aus seinen Worten in Szene I hervorgeht, erscheint diesem auf sein Bitten in der Gestalt einer wunderschönen Frau Seventh Spirit, (appearing in the shape of a beautiful female figure.)                                    Behold!

Man. Oh God! if it be thus and thou
Art not a madness and a mockery,
I yet might be most happy. I will clasp thee,
And we again will be  (The figure vanishes)
My heart is crushed

Dieser Geist ist der Genius Manfred's. Er erscheint hier als wunderschöne Frauengestalt, später im Akt III Scene IV als furchtbarer unterirdischer Dämon. Es heißt hier

**Man.**           Look there, I say,
And steadfastly; -- now tell me what thou
seest?

Albot.    That which should shake me, — but I fear it
not —
I see a dusk and awful figure rise,
Like an infernal god, and his form
Robed as with angry clouds: he stands between
Thyself and me — but I do fear him not.

— — — — —

— — — — —

Alas! lost mortal! what with guests like these
Hast thou to do? I tremble for thy sake:
Why doth he gaze on thee, and thou on him?
Ah! he unveils his aspect: on his brow
The thunder scars are graven, from his eye
Glares forth the immortality of hell —

Daß der Dämon dasselbe ist wie die wunderschöne
Erscheinung in Akt I läßt sich aus folgender Stelle schließen:

Albot.      What art thou unknown being?
answer! speak!

Spirit      The genius of this mortal.

Wie sich Byron dies wirklich vorgestellt hat ist ziemlich
dunkel. Das Motiv hat er wohl ohne weiteres aus der
Vorlage herüber genommen.

Wir erinnern uns hierbei sofort, daß derselbe Geist
Ginotti zuerst als wunderschöne Gestalt und dann als Höllen-
dämon erscheint. Die zweite Erscheinung stimmt mit der in
Manfred vollkommen überein. Ich will zur besseren Ver-
gleichung noch einmal den betreffenden Teil der bereits
angeführten Stelle zu citieren.

— — — I beheld a form more hideous than the
imagination of man is capable of portraying, whose proportions, gigantic and deformed, were seemingly blackened
by the inerasible traces of the thunderbolts of God. —

Der 7te·Geift in Manfred Uft I Scene I, der Dämon
in Uft III Scene IV und first destiny in Uft IV Scene III
find ein und dasfelbe wie fich aus einem Vergleich der
betreffenden Stellen ergiebt. Es folgt fich hierdurch eine
weitere Übereinftimmung. Der Dämon fagt zu Ginotti:

Ah! thou art mine beyond redemption

In gleicher Weife fagt first destiny
Hence! Avaunt! — he's mine.

Byron hat alfo die eine Scene in St. Irvyne in drei
verfchiedene zerlegt. Die letzte Scene in St. Irvyne war
wohl zum Teil Vorbild zur letzten in Manfred. Der Geift
der in „Manfred" erfcheint ift Satan in Perfon. Die Stelle

— — — on his brow
The thunder scars are graven

läßt fich wohl nicht anders erflären und die Stelle in
St. Irvyne, die ihr Vorbild gewefen, weift noch deutlicher
darauf hin. Analog erfcheint dann ebenfalls in der Todes·
fcene in St. Irvyne Luzifer in Perfon. Es heißt hier:

-- — a burst of frightful thunder seemed to
convulse the universal fabric of nature; and, borne on
the pinions of hell's sulphurous whirlwind, he himself
the frightful prince of terror stood before them.

Allerdings ift der tiefgehende Unterfchied zwifchen den
beiden Todesfcenen vorhanden, daß Ginotti für immer der
Macht des Böfen verfallen ift, während Manfred wie Fauft
fie überwindet.

Auch in der Perfönlichfeit und im Charafter der
helden zeigt fich eine entfchiedene Ähnlichfeit zwifchen
Byron's dramatifchem Gedicht und Shelley's Roman. Ginotti
und Manfred find beide durch lange Forfchungen und ge·
heimnisvolle Studien in den Befitz übermenfchlicher Kräfte
gefommen. So fagt Manfred von fich (Uft I, I).

Philosophy and science, and the springs
Of wonder and the wisdom of the world
I have essay'd and in my mind there is
A power to make these subject to itself.

Ähnlich sagt Ginotti von sich:

From my earliest youth — — — curiosity, and a
desire of unveiling the latent mysteries of nature, was
the passion by which all the other emotions of my mind
were intellectually organized. — — — — I then applied
myself to the cultivation of philosophy. — — — —
Natural philosophy at last became the peculiar science
to which I directed my eager inquiries.

Ginotti gelangt in seinen Forschungen sogar dazu, das
Geheimnis ewigen Lebens zu ergründen.

At last during the course of my philosophical inquiries, I ascertained the method by which man might
exist for ever.

Beide haben ihr Wissen teuer, zu teuer erkauft. So
ruft Ginotti aus:

— — — and ah! how dear a price have I paid
for the knowledge.

Und Manfred sagt:

Sorrow is knowledge: they who know the most
Must mourn the deepest o'er the fatal truth.

Es bleibt ihnen nichts zu hoffen und nichts zu
wünschen übrig. So sagt Manfred von sich:

I have no dread,
And feel the curse to have no natural fear,
Nor fluttering throb that beats with hopes or
                                                        wishes
Or lurking love of something of the earth.

Die gleiche Übersättigung läßt sich aus den Worten
Ginotti's schließen:

From my earliest youth before it was quenched
by complete satiation, curiosity etc.

Wie Manfred kennt auch Ginotti nichts, das er lieben
kann:

„Love I cared not fore" sagt er.

Über Manfred wie Ginotti waltet ein dunkles Ver-
hängnis. Der Fluch einer geheimnisvollen, schuldvollen
Vergangenheit lastet auf ihnen und zerstört ihr Leben. Beide
suchen Vergessenheit, können sie aber nicht finden, das Schreck-
gespenst der Ewigkeit, zu der sie verurteilt sind, erfüllt sie
mit Wahnsinn und Verzweiflung. Manfred sagt:

I tell thee man! I have lived many years
Many long years, but they are nothing now
To those which I must number: ages — ages
Space and eternity — and consciousness,
With the fierce thirst of death — and still
unslaked

ferner Akt II, 2                        Forgetfulness
I sought in all, save where 'tis to be found,
And that I have to learn — my sciences,
My long pursued and superhuman art,
Is mortal here — I dwell in my despair
And live — and live for ever.

Den gleichen Gedanken spricht Manfred noch an einer
weiteren Stelle aus:

For hitherto all hateful things conspire
To bind me in existence in a life
Which makes me shrink from immortality
A future like the past.

Manfred ist auf philosophischem Weg zur Überzeugung
seiner ewigen Fortdauer und mit ihr zum Bewußtsein der
ewigen Dauer seiner Qual gekommen. Ginotti ist blos durch
sein Elixir ans Leben gebunden. Er kann dies nun auf
einen andern übertragen und so Ruhe finden. Der Aus-
erwählte ist Wolfstein. Er sagt zu diesem:

To one man alone, Wolfstein, may I communicate
this secret of immortal life: then must I forego my
claim to it, — and oh! with what pleasure shall I
forego it!

Doch scheint Ginotti nach den Schlußworten der Todes-
scene in St. Irvyne die ersehnte Ruhe nicht zu finden; denn
es heißt hier:

Yes, endless existence is thine, Ginotti — a dateless
and hopeless eternity of horror.

Und ob Manfred sie finden wird, ist nach seinen letzten
Worten, obwohl der Höllengeist keine Macht über ihn hat,
zum mindesten fraglich: Er sagt hier

Back to thy hell!
Thou hast no power upon me, that I feel;
Thou never shalt possess me, that I know'!
What I have done, is done; I bear within
A torture which could nothing gain from thine:
The mind which is immortal makes itself
Requital for its good or evil thoughts —
Is its own origin of ill and end

— — — — — — — —
— — — — — — — —

Thou didst not tempt me, and thou couldst not
                                tempt me;
I have not been thy dupe, nor am thy prey —
But was my own destroyer, and will be
My own hereafter. —

Auch Ginotti hat vor seinem Ende das Bewußtsein,
daß seine Qual fortdauern wird. Er sagt:

I am blasted to endless torment.

Nach der schrecklichen Scene am Ende des zweiten
Akts, in der Astarte erscheint und in der Manfreds Verzweiflung ihren Höhepunkt erreicht, ist am Anfang des
dritten Aktes, angesichts der Gewißheit des Endes seines
irdischen Leidens eine sonderbare Ruhe über ihn gekommen.
Es heißt hier:

There is a calm upon me —
Inexplicable stillness! which till now
Did not belong to what I knew of life.

Ebenso geht dem Tode Ginotti's eine dunkle Ver-
zweiflungsscene voraus nach der er dann gefaßten Mutes
dem Tod entgegenfieht; es findet sich allerdings in der
Erzählung von St. Irvyne nur eine Andeutung hievon in
den Worten Ginotti's:

Wolfstein part is past — the hour of agonizing
horror it past; yet the dark and icy gloom of desperation
braces this soul to fortitude.

Dagegen wird in dem Gedicht St. Irvyne's Tower
(1809) eine Scene geschildert, die der in Manfred in mancher
Hinsicht gleicht:

I
How softly through heaven's wide expanse
Bright day's resplendent colour's fade!
How sweetly does the moonbeam's glance
With silver tint St. Irvyne's glade!

II.
No cloud along the spangled air
Is born upon the evening breeze
How solemn is the scene — how fair
The moonbeams rest upon the trees!

III
Yon dark grey turret glimmers white;
Upon it sits the mournful owl;
Along the stillness of the night
Her melancholy shriekings roll.

IV.
But not alone on Irvyne's tower
The silver moon beam pours her ray
It gleams upon the ivied bower,
It dances on the cascade's spray.

V
Ah why do darkening shades conceal
The hour when man must cease to be
Why may not human minds unveil
The dim mists of futurity?

The keenness of the world has torn
The heart which opens to its blast
Despised, neglected, and forlorn
Sinks the wretch in death at last.

Doch hiermit ist die Zahl der Übereinstimmungen
zwischen Manfred und St. Irvyne noch nicht erschöpft.
Einige ganz auffällige Übereinstimmungen finden sich zwischen
der Aftarte Scene in Manfred und der Ballade in Kap II
von Shelley's Roman.

Der einsame Mönch sitzt hier in seiner Zelle, von Todes-
ahnungen durchschauert. Die Geister singen ihm ein Lied
von seiner toten Geliebten. — — — — —

And they sing of the hour
When the stern fates had power
To resolve Rosa's form to its clay.

### III

But that hour is past;
And that hour was the last
Of peace to the dark monk's brain.
— — — — —

— — — — —

### V

Then his eyes wildly roll'd,
When the death bell toll'd
And he rag'd in terrific woe.
— — — — —

### VII

Then he knelt in his cell
And the horrors of hell
Were delights to his agonized pain.

Man vergleiche damit die Art, wie Manfred seine
Verzweiflung schildert.

Daughter of Air! I tell thee, since that hour —
— — — ... — — — — — —
           I have gnashed
My teath in darkness till returning morn,
Then cursed myself till sunset, — I have pray'd
For madness as a blessing

Und

           I have known
The fulness of humiliation, for
I sunk before my own despair. and knelt
To my own desolation.

ferner laffen fich vergleichen die Worte

## VI

And the ice of despair
Chill'd the wild throb of care

und Manfred Att II. 1.

          — now I tremble
And feel a strange cold thaw upon my heart

Es heißt dann weiter in der Ballade:

## VIII

— — — — — — —

A voice hollow and horrible murmur'd around,
„The term of thy penance is done"

## IX

Grew dark the night;
The moon beam bright
Wax'd faint on the mountain high;
And, from the black hill,
Went a voice cold and still, —
Monk thou art free to die

In Byron's Dichtung erfolgen ebenfalls auf den
Ausbruch der Verzweiflung Manfred's als Antwort die
Worte Aftarte's:

Manfred! To morrow ends thine earthly ills.

Ja die Ähnlichkeit zwischen beiden Scenen geht noch
weiter. Der Mönch öffnet den Sarg seiner Geliebten, deren
Geist erscheint und zu ihm spricht wie der Astarte's zu
Manfred.

### XVI

And her skeleton form the dead Nunrear'd,
Which dripped with the chill dew of hell.
In her half-eaten eyeballs two pale flames
      appeared
And triumphant their gleam on the dark, Monk
      glar'd,
As he stood within the cell.

### XVII

And her lank hand lay on his shuddering brain;
But each power was nerv'd by fear. —
I never henceforth may breathe again:
Death now ends mine anguished pain, —
The grave yawns — we meet there.


Auch für die vielumstrittene Stelle in Akt II, 2, wo
Manfred sich des mysteriösen Verbrechens anklagt, giebt es
in St. Irvyne eine Parallelstelle. Es heißt im Manfred:

Manf. — — — — —
   I loved her, and destroy'd her!
Witch     With thy hand
Manf. Not with my hand, but heart — which
      broke her heart —
It gazed on mine, and wither'd. I have shed
Blood, but not hers — and yet her blood was
      shed —
I saw — and could not stanch it.


In Scene 1 desselben Akts sagt Manfred mit Bezug
auf dasselbe geheimnisvolle Verbrechen.


I never quell'd
An enemy, safe in my just defence —
But my embrace was fatal.

Wie bereits angedeutet giebt es eine eigentümliche Parallele hierzu in St. Irvyne. Olympia die Tochter des Grafen della Anzasca ist von grenzenloser Liebe für Wolf= stein erfüllt. Ihre Leidenschaft überwältigt alle die weibliche Zurückhaltung, und sie eilt zu Wolfstein, ihm ihre Liebe zu gestehen. Er weist sie zurück, da er an Megalina gebunden ist. Von enttäuschter Liebe und Leidenschaft überwältigt, sinkt sie besinnungslos zu seinen Füßen nieder. Er hebt sie empor und schließt sie in seine Arme. Während Wolfstein Olympia so in seinen Armen hält, werden beide von Mega= lina überrascht, Olympia stürzt davon, Megalina überhäuft Wolfstein mit Vorwürfen und droht, ihn zu verlassen. Wolfstein wirft sich ihr unter Beteuerungen seiner Unschuld und Liebe zu Füßen. Megalina verlangt als Beweis seiner Liebe die Ermordung Olympias. Nach einigem Sträuben erklärt er sich auch zur That bereit. Mit einem Dolch be= waffnet schleicht er sich nachts in das Gemach der Olympia. Schon hat er den Dolch zum Stoße erhoben, da lächelt Olympia im Schlafe. Wolfstein wird dadurch von seinem mörderischen Vorhaben abgebracht und schleudert den Dolch weit von sich weg. Darüber erwacht Olympia und ist voll Jubel beim Anblick des Geliebten, von dem sie soeben ge= träumt. Sie bittet wiederum um seine Liebe und wird aber= mals von ihm abgewiesen. Verzweifelnd stürzt sie auf den zu Boden liegenden Dolch zu und stößt ihn, ehe Wolfstein ihre Absicht merkt, in ihre Brust. Wolfstein hat sie also nicht mit seiner Hand, sondern mit seinem Herzen getödtet, das ihr Herz brach. Er vergoß nicht ihr Blut und doch ward ihr Blut vergossen. Er sah's und konnt's nicht stillen.

Bevor ich die vorliegende Untersuchung weiter führe muß ich zunächst einiges über das Verhältnis der Figuren von Wolfstein und Ginotti in Shelley's Roman zu sagen. Wie ich glaube, sind sie beide nur Differenzierungen einer und derselben Gestalt, die auch Original zu Byrons Man= fred war. Fassen wir die einzelnen Züge beider zusammen, so erhalten wir eine Gestalt, die mit dem Manfred Byron's fast vollständig übereinstimmt. Daß Ginotti und Wolfstein nur Differenzierungen derselben Urgestalt sind, geht, wie ich glaube, aus folgenden Erwägungen mit Sicherheit hervor:

Die Situation Wolfstein's im ersten Kapitel und die Ginotti's im zehnten Kapitel von St. Irvyne stimmt in den Hauptzügen überein.

Wolfstein übt eine Art Zauber auf seine Gefährten aus:

with him they all asserted that they felt, as it were instinctively impelled to deeds of horror and danger.

Ebenso, nur in noch viel höherem Maße übt Ginotti einen Zauber auf die Räuber aus. Es heißt von ihm (S. 195.)

Every one submitted to Ginotti, for who could resist the superior Ginotti?

Wolfstein und Ginotti lieben es beide nicht den Schleier ihrer Vergangenheit zu lüften. Mit Bezug auf Ginotti wird in St. Irvyne gesagt:

None knew his history — that he concealed within the deepest recesses of his bosom.

Ebenso wenig liebt es Wolfstein über seine Vergangenheit zu reden. Die einzige Antwort auf Megalina's Frage danach ist:

Never question me concerning my past life.

Ähnlich antwortet Manfred auf die Frage des Jägers nach seiner Herkunft ausweichend mit: No matter.

Auch in ihren äußern Gestalt werden beide ähnlich geschildert. Ferner sind sie aus denselben Gründen dazu gekommen den Tod zu fürchten und sich ewige Dauer dieses Lebens zu wünschen. So heißt es von Wolfstein:

his crimes recurred in hideous and disgusting array to the bewildered mind of Wolfstein. To evade death, unconscious why, became an idea on which he dwelt with earnestness.

In gleicher Weise erzählt Ginotti von sich nachdem er seinen Beleidiger vergiftet:

I feared, more than ever, now, to die

Und diese Furcht vor dem Tode hat ihn dazu getrieben nach dem Lebens-Elixir zu forschen. Noch einen andern und letzten Grund für die Identität Wolfstein's und Ginotti's möchte ich anführen, obwohl ihre Zahl damit noch nicht erschöpft ist. Am Schlusse des Romans nimmt Shelley eine kleine Demaskierung seiner geheimnisvollen Persönlichkeit vor indem er uns mitteilt:

Ginotti is Nempere. Eloise is the sister of Wolfstein.

Nun finden sich aber gar keine Andeutungen über ein schwesterliches Verhältnis Eloisen's zu Wolfstein, wohl aber solche aus denen sich auf ein solches zwischen ihr und Ginotti schließen läßt. Hinsichtlich des Eindrucks den Ginotti-Nempere auf Eloise macht heißt es in Kap. VII:

It appeared to her that she had seen him before; that the deep tone of his voice was known to her; and that eye scintillating with a coruscation of mingled sternness and surprise, found some counterpart in herself.

Mutatis mutandis giebt diese Stelle eine Parallele zu der in Manfred Akt II, 2.

She was like me in lineaments etc.

Man hat hieraus schließen wollen daß Manfred's Geliebte seine Schwester ist. Byron spricht das zwar nicht direct aus, immerhin liegt aber diese Vermuthung sehr nahe. Ackermann hat (Anglia Beiblatt VIII S. 15 ff) darauf hingewiesen daß die Idee des Inzestes einen großen Reiz für Shelley hatte. Er weist besonders auf Laon and Cythna hin. Ich möchte noch auf eine andere derartige Stelle aufmerksam machen:

Rosalind and Helen 150 ff.

— — — he told
That a hellish shape at midnight led
The ghost of a youth with hoary hair
And sate on the seat beside him there,
Till a naked child came wandering by
When the fiend would change to a lady fair.
A fearful tale. The truth was worse
For here a sister and a brother
Had solemnized a monstruous curse

Meeting in this fair solitude:
For beneath yon very skyn
Had they resigned to one another
Body and soul.

Neben dem Motio des Inzests haben wir das daß der Dämon eine schöne Frauengestalt annimmt. Aller Wahr= scheinlichkeit nach hat also Byron diese beiden Motive von Shelley.

Ist nun Ginotti=Nempere und Wolfstein in der ursprünglichen Erzählung identisch, so wird die Ähnlichkeit mit Manfred noch größer.

Die Scene in der Nempere seine Verführungskünste versucht, hat große Ähnlichkeit mit der berühmten zwischen Faust und Gretchen. Es sei mir deshalb gestattet sie anzu= führen.

„Why" said Nempere „are we thought to believe that the union of two who love each other is wicked, unless authorized by certain rites and ceremonials, which certainly cannot change the tenour of sentiments which it is destined that these two people should entertain of each other.

It is, I suppose, answered Eloise calmly, because God has willed it so; besides, continued she blushing at she knew' not what „it would".

„And is then the superior and towering soul of Eloise subjected to sentiments and prejudices so stale and vulgar as these?" interrupted Nempere indignantly. „Say, do you not think it an insult to two souls, united to each other in the irrefragable covenants of love and congeniality, to promise, in the sight of a Beeing whom they know not, that fidelity which is certain otherwise?

But I do know that Being! cried Eloise with warmth and when I cease to know him may I die!

I pray to him every morning and, when I kneel at night I thank him for the mercy which, he has shown to a poor friendless girl like me! He is the protector of the friendless, and I love and adore him.

Man vergleiche hierzu noch folgende Stelle aus Rosalind and Helen 342 ff.

We will have rites our faith to bind
But our church shall be the starry night

Our altar the grassy earth outspread
And our priest the muttering wind.

Es erinnert dies sofort an Manfreds Worte:

bound by ties
Stronger than the church links withall.

Ähnlich wie wir durch Kombination von Ginotti·
Nempere und Wolfstein den Ur·Manfred erhalten, erhalten wir
durch Kombination von Victoria·Olympia, Eloise und
der Nonne in der Ballade des zweiten Kapitels die Ur·
Astarte.

Daß Victoria und Olympia dasselbe sind, geht
unmittelbar aus dem Vergleich der beiden Stellen hervor:

'T was then that her form on the whirlwind
upholding,
The ghost of the murder'd Victoria strode

und

and the bleeding image of the murdered
Olympia — haunted him -  —

Ich glaube annehmen zu dürfen, daß die dunkle That
von deren Erinnerung Wolfstein am Anfang von St. Irvyne
gequält wird in der ursprünglichen Erzählung identisch
ist mit der Ermordung Olympia's. Allerdings wird dann
die Reihenfolge der Ereignisse umgekehrt. Aber gerade
dadurch wird die Verzweiflung Wolfstein's im ersten Kapitel
besser erklärt. Die Ballade im Kap. II läßt sich leicht in
denselben Zusammenhang bringen. Es ist als ob Shelley
sich von dem geheimnisvollen Grundmotiv der Erzählung
nicht hätte trennen können. Was dann die Einheitlichkeit
der Gestalt Victoria·Olympia·Nonne und der Eloisen's
anbetrifft so finden sich allerdings in Shelley's Roman keine
Andeutungen dafür, aber ich glaube sie schon aus dem
Grund annehmen zu können da ihre Kombination Byron's
Astarte ergiebt.

Außerdem will ich noch auf einige weitere, allerdings
unbedeutendere Züge der Übereinstimmung zwischen Byron's
dramatischer Dichtung und Shelley's Roman hinweisen die
immerhin noch zur Stütze der aufgestellten Hypothese dienen
können.

Bezüglich Wolfstein's Abstammung wird gesagt:

Ah! that eventful existence whose fate had dragged
the heir of a wealthy potentate, in Germany — — —

und von Manfred heißt es:

Thy garb and gait bespeak thee of high lineage,
One of the many chiefs, whose castled crags
Look over the lower valley. — Which of these
May call thee lord?

Das Schloß Manfreds liegt in der Nähe eines Klosters
wie aus dem Erscheinen des Abtes hervorgeht. Im Kap. I
von St. Irvyne ist gleichfalls von einem dem Schauplatz
der Erzählung benachbarten Kloster die Rede, und weiterhin
spielt eine verfallene Abtei eine gewisse Rolle. Ein weiteres
ähnliches Motiv ließe vielleicht sich noch darin sehen
daß Ginotti wie Manfred unter dem Ausdruck des Ent-
setzens den angebotenen Trunk Wein zurückweisen. Die
Scene aus Manfred ist bekannt, in St. Irvyne heißt es:

Do you not drink?
No replied Ginotti sullenly.
A pause ensued; during which the eyes of Ginotti,
glaring with demoniacal scintillations, spoke tenfold
terrors to the soul of Wolfstein.

Die Übereinstimmung mit der Scene in Manfred wird
noch besonders dadurch auffallend, daß wie dort Manfred
der Frage des Jägers nach seiner Herkunft ausweicht, hier
Ginotti eine solche von vorneherein abschneidet. Er sagt:

My name, my family, and the circumstances which
have attended my career through existence, it neither
boots you to know, nor me to declare.

Ich bin vielleicht zu weit gegangen in dem Bestreben
Übereinstimmungen zwischen Manfred und St. Irvyne heraus-
zufinden. Aber selbst dies zugegeben bin ich fest überzeugt,
daß höchst auffallende und unleugbare Parallelen zwischen
Manfred und St. Irvyne bestehen, die ein interessantes
Streiflicht auf verschiedene dunkle Stellen im Manfred
werfen. Ich glaube die Manfred-Frage, wenn auch
nicht gelöst, so doch den Weg zu ihrer Lösung gezeigt
zu haben und überlasse es berufeneren Federn die letzten

Konsequenzen aus den von mir gegebenen Thatsachen zu ziehen.

Daß Byron St. Irvyne gekannt haben muß, ergiebt sich noch aus folgendem. Ein weiteres Motiv aus St. Irvyne findet sich in einer andern Dichtung Byron's nämlich im Deformed, Transformed.

Die Räuber denen sich Wolfstein angeschlossen hat, haben einen Raubanfall auf einen italienischen Grafen geplant. Wolfstein versäumt die Unternehmung. Als er zurückkommt erfährt er, daß der Anschlag ausgeführt, der Graf getötet ist, und seine Tochter in der Gewalt der Räuber. Er verliebt sich in sie, tritt den Räubern gegenüber als ihr Beschützer auf und um sie vor den Werbungen Cavigni's zu retten vergiftet er diesen. Seine Geliebte und er entkommen dann durch den geheimnisvollen Beistand Ginotti's der Rache der Räuber.

Eine ähnliche Rolle spielt Arnold im Deformed Transformed gegenüber Olympia. Diese ist von einem Haufen Soldaten bedroht. Arnold kommt und befreit sie mit mit eigener Lebensgefahr. Ihre Schönheit bezaubert ihn und es gelingt ihm dann auch nach den Andeutungen des Chors in Teil III ihre Liebe zu gewinnen. Wie Wolfgang der geheimnisvolle Einfluß Ginotti's zur Seite steht, so steht Arnold der Cäsars zur Seite.

Eine ziemlich wörtliche Parallele findet sich noch zwischen einer Stelle in St. Irvyne (S. 169), wo ein Räuber von vielen wackern Gesellen spricht who otherwise would have been ornaments to their country in peace, thunderbolts to their enemies in war

und Deformed Transformed I 1 wo von Demetrius Poliorketes gesagt wird

> The shame
> Of Greece in peace, her thunderbolt in war.

Vielleicht ist auch die schon behandelte Übereinstimmung in der Schilderung des Gewitters in C H III mit der im ersten Kapitel von St. Irvyne hier einzureihen.

# Benützte Bücher.

The works of P. B. Shelley edited by H. B. Forman, London 1876—80.

The poetical works of P. B. Shelley. Rossetti, London 1870.

Moore, Byron's works and life. London 1873.

The works of Lord Byron, Tauchnitz Ausgabe. Leipzig 1866.

Kölbing, Byron Ausgabe 1, 2, Weimar 1896.

Elze, Lord Byron, Berlin 1886.

Donner Lord Byron's Weltanschauung, Helsingfors 1897.

Life of Lord Byron by R. Noel, London 1890.

Life of P. B. Shelley by W. Sharp, London 1887.

Dowden, Life of Shelley, London 1886.

The works of William Wordsworth edited by W. Knight, London 1896.

Byron by John Nicholl, London 1888.

Shelley by Jd. Symonds, London 1887.